Cute & Easy
CROCHET WITH FLOWERS

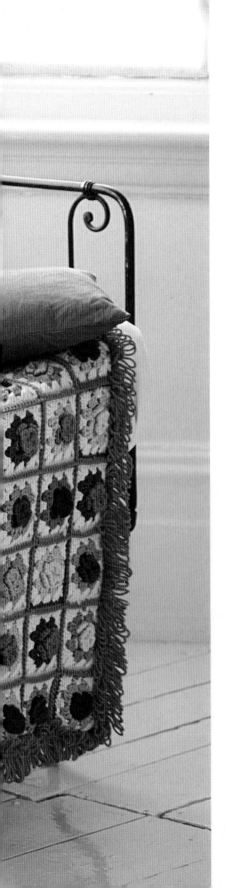

Cute & Easy
CROCHET with FLOWERS

35 beautiful projects using floral motifs

Nicki Trench

CICO BOOKS
LONDON NEW YORK

Published in 2013 by CICO Books
An imprint of Ryland Peters & Small
20–21 Jockey's Fields, London WC1R 4BW
519 Broadway, 5th Floor, New York NY 10012
www.rylandpeters.com

10 9 8 7 6 5 4 3 2 1

Text copyright © Nicki Trench 2013
Design, photography, and illustration copyright
© CICO Books 2013

A CIP catalogue record for this book is available
from the British Library.

UK ISBN: 978-1-78249-049-4

Printed in China

EDITOR: Marie Clayton
DESIGNER: Louise Turpin
ARTWORKS: Stephen Dew and Kate Simunek
PHOTOGRAPHER: Caroline Arber
STYLIST: Sophie Martell

Contents

Introduction

This book has been an absolute delight to work on. The theme is floral so I have used flowers and petals, either incorporated into the patterns or added as an edging or decoration. Crochet is the perfect craft for making flowers because it lends itself to combining shapes and colours.

There are projects suitable for all levels so if you want to try a project and you find the flowers are a little more challenging, just replace them with an easier version from another project. We have organised the patterns into Beginner, Intermediate and Experienced chapters to give you a guide. If you are just starting out, try the gorgeous Poppy Purse, Tote Bag, Floral-edged Jam Pot Covers or the Baby Beanie Hat. For those who feel more confident, try the beautiful Gypsy Queen Throw, Floral Shell Stitch Cushion Cover or Beaded Craft Kit Roll, or we even have a simple cover for your Kindle or iPad. More experienced crocheters will love the challenge of the Buggy Blanket, Shelf Edging or Blossom Necklace.

There are projects for all seasons and occasions – the Tea Cosy is a fabulous centrepiece to put on top of the pretty cotton Tablecloth for a summer picnic and the scarves and throws will brighten up any dull winter's day. Some of the projects are there just for the pure joy of crochet: try the Oven Cloths or Pansy and Kittens.

I've tried to use colours and stitches to inspire and lure you into making lots of things in the book, but feel free to pick and choose your flowers from the many patterns and to swap and change the colours to suit your choice.

Cute & Easy Crochet with Flowers has an excellent techniques section with clear illustrations and instructions to guide you through the basic stitch techniques. When making flowers the sewing in of the ends is vital; it will make the world of difference to have a good yarn sewing needle to close centre holes and to weave the ends in to neaten up the petals.

Whatever projects you make in this book, I'm sure you'll not be disappointed and I hope you have as much fun crocheting as I did designing the patterns for your delight.

Crochet Know-how

If you're unsure how to make a particular crochet stitch, look in this section where you'll find beautifully clear illustrated crochet techniques. There are instructions on how to make basic stitches, clusters and beading.

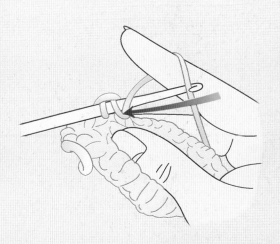

Techniques

In this section, we explain how to master the simple crochet techniques that you need to make the projects in this book.

Holding the hook

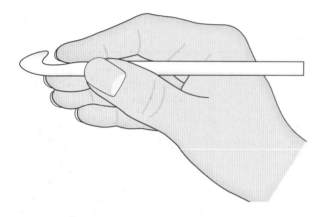

Pick up your hook as though you are picking up a pen or pencil. Keeping the hook held loosely between your fingers and thumb, turn your hand so that the palm is facing up and the hook is balanced in your hand and resting in the space between your index finger and your thumb.

Holding the yarn

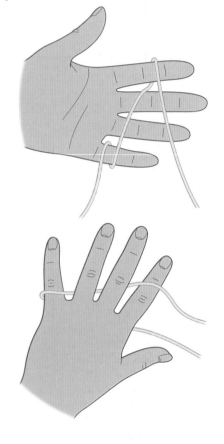

1 Pick up the yarn with your little finger in the opposite hand to your hook, with your palm facing upwards and with the short end in front. Turn your hand to face downwards, with the yarn on top of your index finger and under the other two fingers and wrapped right around the little finger, as shown right.

2 Keeping your index finger only at a slight curve, hold your work or the slip knot using the same hand, between your middle finger and your thumb and just below the crochet hook and loop/s on the hook.

Making a slip knot

The simplest way is to make a circle with the yarn, so that the loop is facing downwards.

1 In one hand hold the circle at the top where the yarn crosses, and let the tail drop down at the back so that it falls across the centre of the loop. With your free hand or the tip of a crochet hook, pull a loop through the circle.

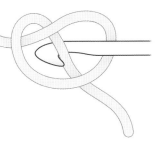

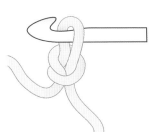

2 Put the hook into the loop and pull gently so that it forms a loose loop on the hook.

Yarn round hook (yrh)

To create a stitch, you'll need to catch the yarn with the hook and pull it through the loop. Holding your yarn and hook correctly, catch the yarn from behind with the hook pointing upwards. As you gently pull the yarn through the loop on the hook, turn the hook so that it faces downwards and slide the yarn through the loop. The loop on the hook should be kept loose enough for the hook to slide through easily.

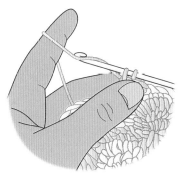

Chain (ch)

1 Using the hook, wrap the yarn round the hook and pull it through the loop on the hook, creating a new loop on the hook. Continue in this way to create a chain of the required length.

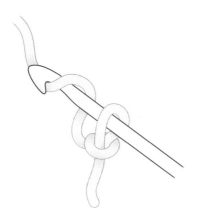

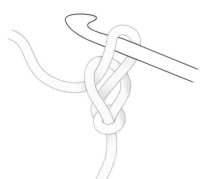

2 Keep moving your middle finger and thumb close to the hook, to hold the work in place with the opposite hand that you hold your hook with.

Tip

Always bring the hook back to face upwards, turning the hook downwards (not sideways) as it slips through the loop/s on the hook.

Chain ring/circle

If you are crocheting a round shape, one way of starting off is by crocheting a number of chains following the instructions in your pattern, and then joining them into a circle.

1 To join the chain into a circle, insert the crochet hook into the first chain that you made (not into the slip knot), yarn round hook, then pull the yarn through the chain and through the loop on your hook at the same time, thereby creating a slip stitch and forming a circle.

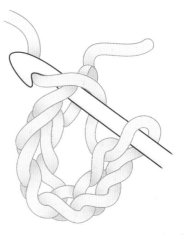

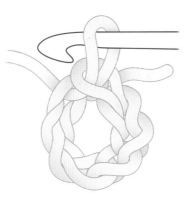

2 You will now have a circle ready according to your pattern.

Some of the circles in this book have been made by creating a spiral, whereby you make two chains and insert your hook into the second chain from the hook (the first chain you made). Following the instructions in the pattern will then ensure the spiral has the correct amount of stitches. It's essential to use a stitch marker when using this method, so that you know where to start and finish your round.

Chain space (ch sp)

1 A chain space is the space that has been made under a chain in the previous round or row, and falls in between other stitches.

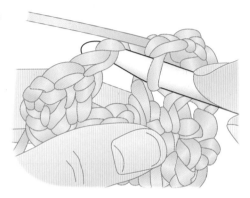

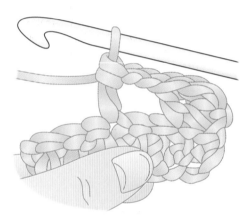

2 Stitches into a chain space are made directly into the hole created under the chain and not into the chain stitches themselves.

Making rounds

When working in rounds the work is not turned, so you are always working from one side. Depending on the pattern you are working, a 'round' can be square. You may need to make a turning chain to create the height you need for the stitch you are working, as listed under making rows (right). Or, you may work in a spiral, in which case you do not need a turning chain.

To keep count of where you are in the pattern, you will need to place a stitch marker at the beginning of each round; a piece of yarn in a contrasting colour is useful for this. Loop the stitch marker into the first stitch; when you have made a round and reached the point where the stitch marker is, work this stitch, take out the stitch marker from the previous round and put it back into the first stitch of the new round.

Making rows

When making straight rows you need to make a turning chain to create the height you need for the stitch you are working with, as follows:
Double crochet = 1 chain
Half treble = 2 chain
Treble = 3 chain
Double treble = 4 chain
Triple treble = 5 chain
Quadruple treble = 6 chain

Joining new yarn

If using double crochet, insert the hook as normal into the stitch, using the original yarn, and pull a loop through. Drop the old yarn and pick up the new yarn. Wrap the new yarn round the hook and pull it through the two loops on the hook.

Slip stitch

A slip stitch doesn't create any height and is often used as the last stitch to create a smooth and even round or row.

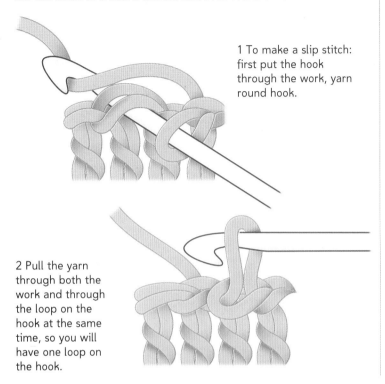

1 To make a slip stitch: first put the hook through the work, yarn round hook.

2 Pull the yarn through both the work and through the loop on the hook at the same time, so you will have one loop on the hook.

Double crochet (dc)

1 Insert the hook into your work, yarn round hook and pull the yarn through the work only. You will then have two loops on the hook.

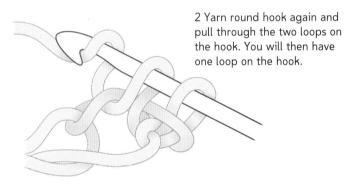

2 Yarn round hook again and pull through the two loops on the hook. You will then have one loop on the hook.

Half treble (htr)

1 Before inserting the hook into the work, wrap the yarn round the hook and put the hook through the work with the yarn wrapped around.

2 Yarn round hook again and pull through the first loop on the hook (you now have three loops on the hook).

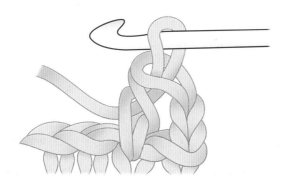

3 Yarn round hook and pull the yarn through all three loops. You will be left with one loop on the hook.

Treble (tr)

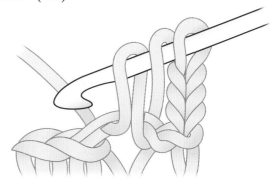

1 Before inserting the hook into the work, wrap the yarn round the hook and put the hook through the work with the yarn wrapped around.

2 Yarn round hook again and pull through the first loop on the hook (you now have three loops on the hook). Yarn round hook again, pull the yarn through two loops (you now have two loops on the hook).

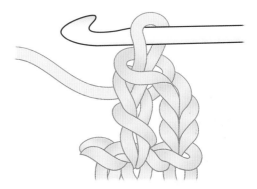

3 Pull the yarn through two loops again. You will be left with one loop on the hook.

Double treble (dtr)

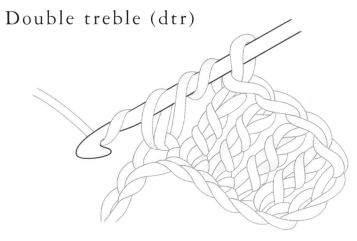

Yarn round hook twice, insert hook into the stitch, yarn round hook, pull a loop through (four loops on hook), yarn round hook, pull the yarn through two stitches (three loops on hook), yarn round hook, pull a loop through the next two stitches (two loops on hook), yarn round hook, pull a loop through the last two stitches.

Triple treble (trtr)

Yarn round hook three times, insert hook into the stitch, yarn round hook, pull a loop through (five loops on hook), yarn round hook, pull the yarn through two stitches (four loops on hook), yarn round hook, pull a loop through the next two stitches (three loops on hook), yarn round hook, pull a loop through the next two stitches (two loops on hook), yarn round hook, pull a loop through the last two stitches.

Tip
When working on clusters, keep the loops loose on the hook and pull the yarn through carefully to avoid splitting the yarn.

Cluster (CL)

Working two or more part stitches and taking them together at the top to make one stitch gives a cluster in a stitch pattern or a decrease when working a fabric. The example shows making a cluster by taking three trebles (3trCL) together.

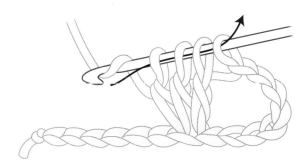

Leaving the last loop of each stitch on the hook, work a treble into each of the next three stitches, thus making four loops on the hook. Yarn round hook and pull through all four loops to join the stitches together at the top and make one loop on the hook.

Popcorn

This kind of bobble is made from complete stitches. The example shows four trebles worked in a chain space and taken together, but a popcorn can be placed in any stitch and be made up of any practical number or combination of stitches.

1 Inserting the hook in the same place each time, work four complete trebles (see page 16).

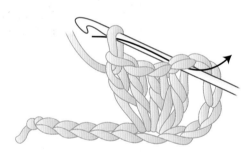

2 Slip the hook out of the last loop.

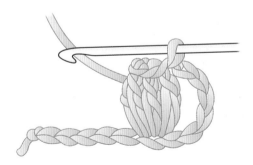

3 Insert the hook into the top of the first stitch, then into the last loop, yarn round hook and pull through.

Threading beads onto yarn

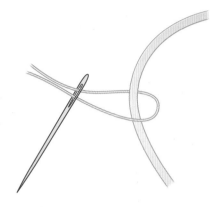

1 Make a loop in some cotton sewing thread and thread a sewing needle with the loop (not the end). Leave the loop hanging approx 2.5cm (1in) from the eye of the needle. Pull the yarn end through the loop of the thread.

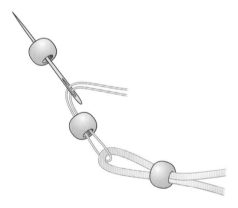

2 Thread the beads (two or three at a time), onto the sewing needle, pushing them down onto the strand of the yarn. Continue to thread beads until the required number is reached.

Place a bead

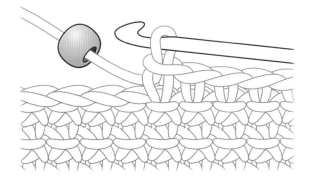

1 Thread all the beads needed onto the yarn before commencing work. When a bead is needed, slide it up against the back of the work.

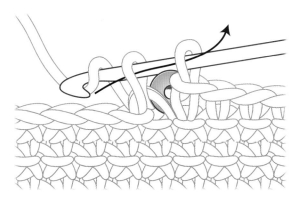

2 Work the stitch as indicated in the pattern, securing the bead in place.

Increasing

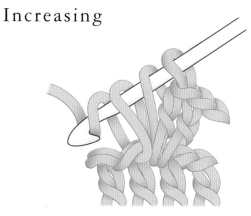

Make two or three stitches into one stitch from the previous row. The illustration shows a two-stitch increase being made.

Decreasing

You can decrease by either missing the next stitch and continuing to crochet, or by crocheting two or more stitches together. The basic technique for crocheting stitches together is the same, no matter which stitch you are using. The following examples show dc2tog, dc3tog, htr2tog and tr3tog.

Double crochet 2 stitches together (dc2tog)

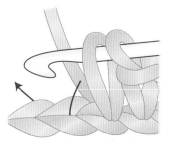

1 Insert the hook into your work, yarn round hook and pull the yarn through the work. You will then have two loops on the hook.

2 Yarn round hook again and pull through the two loops on the hook. You will then have one loop on the hook.

Double crochet 3 stitches together (dc3tog)

Work as for dc2tog until there are three loops on the hook; insert hook into the next stitch, yarn round hook, pull yarn through (four loops on hook), yarn round hook and pull through all the loops; one loop left on the hook.

Half treble 2 stitches together (htr2tog)

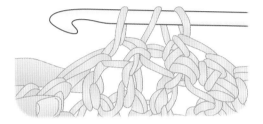

1 Yarn round hook, insert hook into next stitch, yarn round hook, draw yarn through (three loops on the hook).

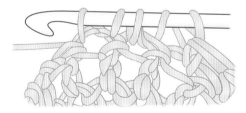

2 Yarn round hook, insert hook into next stitch, yarn round hook, draw yarn through.

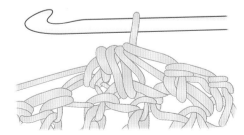

3 Draw yarn through all five loops on the hook.

Treble 3 stitches together (tr3tog)

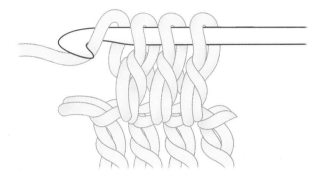

Work a treble into each of the next three stitches as normal, but leave the last loop of each stitch on the hook (four loops on the hook). Yarn round hook and pull the yarn through all the stitches on the hook to join them together. You will finish with one loop on the hook.

How to double crochet squares together

Place two squares wrong sides together, lining them up so that the stitches on each square match. Put the hook through the top loops of the first square and also through the corresponding top loops of the second square. Join in the yarn, make 1 chain, insert the hook into the top stitches of both squares and make a double crochet seam across the top of the squares.

Tip

If you are making lots of small motifs sew in the ends as you complete each one – doing it all at the end will be time consuming and boring.

Fastening off

Cut the yarn, leaving a tail of approx 10cm (4in). Pull the tail all the way through the last loop.

Break yarn

Do not fasten off. Simply cut the yarn approx 10cm (4in) from the work and leave a loop on the hook.

Sewing in ends

Thread a yarn sewing needle with a large enough eye to thread the yarn through. Weave ends in and out of the work approx 5cm (2in) on the wrong side, keeping to the same colour.

Starching

If you're working with flowers or projects that curl or the project needs to be hung up, using spray starch helps keep its shape. First, block the piece to achieve the correct shape and spray starch over the top of the piece. Take a cloth, such as a cotton or linen tea towel, place this over the top and lightly press. Leave to dry.

Chapter 1
Starting Out

There are some perfect beginner-level projects in this chapter, which use basic stitches to practise your crochet skills. Try the Kindle Cover (page 28), Egg Cosies (page 46), Poppy Purse (page 26) or the Rose Headband (page 34). Pansy and Kittens (page 56) and the Egg Cosies are great for learning to crochet in the round.

MATERIALS

Rooster Almerino Aran (50% baby alpaca/50% merino wool) Aran (worsted) yarn
- 1 x 50g (1¾oz) ball – approx 94m (103yd) – of 305 Custard (**A**)
- Small amounts of DK (light worsted) yarn in black (**B**), red (**C**) and green (**D**)
- 4.5mm (US size 7) and 3.5mm (US size E/4) crochet hooks
- Yarn sewing needle
- 25.5 x 35.5cm (10 x 14in) piece of lining fabric
- Sewing needle and matching thread
- 1 x 2cm (¾in) button

ABBREVIATIONS

ch   chain
dc   double crochet
dtr   double treble
htr   half treble
rep   repeat
RS   right side
sp(s) space(s)
ss   slip stitch
st(s) stitch(es)
WS   wrong side
yrh   yarn round hook

SPECIAL ABBREVIATIONS

dc2tog (double crochet 2 stitches together) – [insert hook in next st, yrh, pull yarn through] twice, yrh, pull through all 3 loops on hook (one stitch decreased).

htrCL (half treble cluster) – [yrh, insert hook in ring, pull yarn through] twice, yrh, pull yarn through all 5 loops on hook.

MEASUREMENTS

Approx 15 x 10cm (6 x 4in)

TENSION

15½ sts x 18 rows over a 10cm (4in) square working double crochet using 4.5mm (US size 7) hook and A.

Poppy Purse

This pretty purse could be used for money, but also for make-up or even your crochet hooks and scissors.

Purse

Using A and 4.5mm (US size 7) hook, make 24ch.
ROW 1: 1dc in 2nd ch from hook, 1dc in each ch to end. (23 sts)
ROW 2: 1ch, 1dc in each st. (23 sts)
Rep Row 2 until work measures approx 19cm (7½in).
Make flap:
ROWS 1–8: 1ch, dc2tog, 1dc in each st to end. (15 sts)
ROW 9: 1ch, dc2tog, 1dc in each of next 4 sts, dc2tog, 1dc in each of next 5 sts, dc2tog. (12 sts)
Make buttonhole:
ROW 1: 1ch, dc2tog, 1dc in each of next 3 sts, 2ch, miss 2 sts, 1dc in each of next 3 sts, dc2tog.
ROW 2 (RS): 1ch, dc2tog, 1dc in each of next 2 sts, 2dc in 2ch sp, 1dc in each of next 2 sts, dc2tog. (8 sts)
Do not fasten off, but work edging as follows.
Work edging:
1ch, work 44dc evenly along one side edge, 3dc in corner st (47 sts), 22dc along bottom edge (69 sts), 3dc in corner st (72 sts), 44dc along second side edge (116 sts), 3dc in corner st (119 sts), 8dc along top edge (127 sts), join with ss in first 1ch.
Fasten off.

Poppies

(MAKE 2)
Using B and 3.5mm (US size E/4) hook and leaving a long tail, make 6ch, join with a ss in first ch to form a ring.
ROUND 1: 2ch, [1htrCL in ring, 1ch] 12 times, join with a ss in back loop of top of first htrCL. (12 htrCL)
Break off B, but do not fasten off.

ROUND 2: Working in back loops of sts only, join in C, 3ch (counts as 1dc, 2ch), 1dc in top of next htrCL from previous round, *2ch, 1dc in top of next htrCL; rep from * to end of round, ending 2ch, join with a ss in first of 3ch. (12 dc)
ROUND 3: Working in back loops of sts only, *4ch (counts as first dtr), [1dtr in each of next 2 ch, 1dtr in next dc] 3 times, 1dtr in each of next 2 ch, 4ch (counts as 1dtr), 1ss in base of last dtr, 1ss in next dc (13 dtr, 1 petal made); rep from * twice more, working last ss in base of first 4ch of first petal. (3 petals made)
Fasten off.
Weave B yarn tail around centre hole, pull to close and secure. Neaten petals as you sew in remaining ends.

Lining

Block crocheted piece. Cut a piece of lining fabric the same size and shape as purse allowing an extra 1.5cm (5/8in) seam allowance all around. Fold under the seam allowances all around the lining piece, then pin, press and machine or hand sew in place. Make a buttonhole on lining to correspond with buttonhole position on crocheted piece.

Finishing

With WS together, pin lining onto crocheted piece. Hand sew lining in place, making sure buttonhole positions match. With RS of lining facing, turn up bottom edge to align with start of flap shaping. Using a length of yarn, sew side seams of purse, leaving flap open. Sew on button to correspond with buttonhole.
Attach one poppy to centre of front flap and one poppy to top left-hand corner on back of purse.
Using D, embroider a stalk for each poppy in chain stitch.

MATERIALS

COVER
Rooster Almerino Baby (50% baby alpaca/50% merino wool)

- 1 x 50g (1¾oz) ball – approx 125m (136½yd) – of 511 Anemone (**MC**)

FLOWERS AND LEAVES
- Scraps of yarn (of same weight as MC) in red (**A**), bright pink (**B**), white (**C**) and green (**D**)

- 3mm (US size D/3) crochet hook
- 21 x 33cm (8¼ x 13in) piece of lining fabric
- Yarn sewing needle
- Sewing needle and thread to match lining
- 80cm (32in) red ribbon 1.5cm (⅝in) wide

ABBREVIATIONS

ch	chain
dc	double crochet
rep	repeat
RS	right side
ss	slip stitch
st(s)	stitch(es)
WS	wrong side

MEASUREMENTS
Approx 18 x 13.5cm (7 x 5¼in)

TENSION
22 sts x 25 rows over a 10cm (4in) square working double crochet using 3mm (US size D/3) hook and MC.

NOTE
Measure the length and the width of the device. This pattern is based on a Kindle device measuring approx 17 x 11.7 x 0.9cm (6¾ x 4¾ x ⅜in), but use the tension as a guide to make a base chain to measure the width of your device and continue until the length matches the length of your device. If your device is much bigger than 17 x 11.7 x 0.9cm (6¾ x 4¾ x ⅜in) you will need more yarn.

Kindle Cover

I made this for a Paperwhite Kindle, but the pattern can easily be adjusted to make a cover for any device, including a mobile phone, tablet or laptop.

Front and Back

(MAKE 2 THE SAME)
Using MC, make 31ch.
ROW 1: 1dc in 2nd ch from hook, 1dc in each ch to end. (30 dc)
ROW 2: 1ch (does NOT count as a st), 1dc in each dc to end. (30 dc)
Rep Row 2 until work measures 18cm (7in). Fasten off.

Flowers

(MAKE 1 IN EACH OF A, B AND C)
Make 4ch, join with a ss in first ch to form a ring.
ROUND 1 (RS): [5ch, 1ss in ring] 5 times. (5 petals)
Fasten off.

Leaves

(MAKE 1 IN D)
Make 8ch, join with a ss in first ch to form a ring.
ROUND 1 (RS): [6ch, 1dc in 2nd ch from hook, 1dc in each of next 4 ch, 1ss in ring] 4 times. (4 leaves)
Fasten off.

Lining

Cut the lining fabric into two pieces, each 21 x 16.5cm (8¼ x 6½in). If the cover is for a different device, measure the length, width and depth to determine the length and width of the finished cover. Then add another 3.5cm (1³/₈in) to both dimensions

and cut two pieces of lining fabric to these measurements.
Place the lining pieces RS together and pin along sides and bottom edges. Sew the sides and bottom with a 1.5cm (⁵/₈in) seam. Press seams open.
Fold 1.5cm (⁵/₈in) to WS along top edge and press.

Finishing

Block and steam front and back to make them the same size.
Block the leaves, grouping them to one side of the ring.
Sew in all ends.
Place the front and back crochet pieces RS together and join side and bottom seams using MC and yarn sewing needle. Turn RS out.
Place the lining inside the crochet piece WS together. Pin and hand sew the top edge of the lining to the top edge of the crochet piece using a sewing needle and a matching colour thread.
Sew the leaves and then the flowers onto the front of the cover.
Cut the ribbon in half and sew one end in the centre of the top edge of the lining on either side.

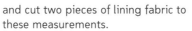

MATERIALS

BAG
Cascade 220 (100% Peruvian highland wool)
Aran (worsted) yarn
- 2 x 100g (3½oz) hanks – approx 400m (440yd) – of 8902 Herb (**A**)

EDGING
Rooster Almerino DK (50% baby alpaca/50% merino wool) DK (light worsted) yarn
- 1 x 50g (1¾oz) ball – approx 112.5m (124yd) – of 201 Cornish (**B**)

FLOWERS
Rooster Baby (100% fine merino wool)
- Small amount of 410 Liquorice (**C**)
Rooster Almerino DK (50% baby alpaca/50% merino wool) DK (light worsted) yarn
- Small amount each of 201 Cornish (**D**), 220 Lighthouse (**E**), 215 Lilac Sky (**F**), 211 Brighton Rock (**G**), 210 Custard (**H**)

- 3.5mm (US size E/4) and 4mm (US size G/6) crochet hooks
- 85 x 45cm (34 x 18in) lining fabric
- Sewing needle and matching thread

ABBREVIATIONS

beg	beginning
ch	chain
cont	continu(e)(ing)
dc	double crochet
dtr	double treble
rep	repeat
RS	right side
sp(s)	space(s)
ss	slip stitch
st(s)	stitch(es)
tr	treble
trtr	triple treble
WS	wrong side

MEASUREMENTS
25 x 23 x 11cm (9¾ x 9½ x 4¼in) including top edging

TENSION
17 sts x 20 rows over a 10cm (4in) square working double crochet using 3.5mm (US size E/4) hook.

Tote Bag

A great size for a bag – it's big enough for essentials or you can use it to store all those balls of yarn.

Front/Back

(MAKE 2)
Using A and 3.5mm (US size E/4) hook, make 43ch.
ROW 1: 1dc in 2nd ch from hook, 1dc in each ch to end of row. (42 dc)
ROW 2: 1ch, 1dc in each dc to end. Rep Row 2 until work measures approx

21.5cm (8½in).
Fasten off.

Sides

(MAKE 2)
Using A and 3.5mm (US size E/4) hook, make 18ch.

size E/4) hook, join yarn with a ss in seam at beg of top of Front, make 1ch, 1dc in same place as ss, then counting each dc along top edge as a st (42 sts across Front and Back, 17 sts across each Side) and each seam as a st (4 seams) work as follows – *1ch, miss 1 st, 1dc in next st; rep from * to last st, 1ch, miss 1 st, join with a ss in first dc. (61 ch sps)
Cont with RS facing.
ROUND 2: 1ch, 1dc in first ch sp, *1ch, miss next ch sp, [2dtr, 4ch, 1ss in first of 4ch, 2dtr] in next ch sp, 1ch, miss next ch sp, 1dc in next ch sp; rep from * to last 2 ch sps, miss 2 ch sps, join with a ss in first dc.
Fasten off.

Small Flowers

(MAKE 1 EACH IN E, F, G AND H)
Using C and 3.5mm (US size E/4) hook, make 4ch, join with a ss in first ch to form a ring.
ROUND 1 (RS): 1ch, 6dc in ring, break off C, join in D with a ss in first dc. (6 dc)
Cont in rounds with RS always facing.
ROUND 2: 1ch, 2dc in each st to end, break off D, join in E, F, G or H with a ss in first dc. (12 dc)
ROUND 3: *3ch, 2tr in next st, 3ch, 1ss in next st; rep from * to end, join with a ss at base of first 3ch. (6 petals)
Fasten off.

Large Flower

(MAKE 2)
Using C and 4mm (US size G/6), make 4ch, join with a ss in first ch to form a ring.
ROUND 1 (RS): 1ch, 6dc in ring, break off C, join in G with a ss in first dc. (6 dc)
Cont in rounds with RS always facing.
ROUND 2: 1ch, 2dc in each st to end, join with a ss in first dc. (12 dc)
ROUND 3: 1ch, 2dc in each st to end, break off G, join in B with a ss in first dc. (24 dc)
ROUND 4: *5ch, 1trtr in each of next 3 sts, 5ch, 1ss in next st; rep from * to end, join with a ss at base of first 5ch. (6 petals)
Fasten off.

ROW 1: 1dc in 2nd ch from hook, 1dc in each ch to end of row. (17 dc)
ROW 2: 1ch, 1dc in each dc to end.
Rep Row 2 until work measures approx 21.5cm (8½in) or to match Front/Back.
Fasten off.

Base

(MAKE 1)
Using A and 3.5mm (US size E/4) hook, make 43ch.
ROW 1: 1dc in 2nd ch from hook, 1dc in each ch to end of row. (42 dc)
ROW 2: 1ch, 1dc in each dc to end.
Rep Row 2 until work measures approx 11cm (4¼in).
Fasten off.

Handles

(MAKE 2)
Using A and 3.5mm (US size E/4) hook, make 7ch.
ROW 1: 1dc in 2nd ch from hook, 1dc in each of next 5 ch. (6 dc)
ROWS 2–60: 1ch, 1dc in each dc to end.
Fasten off.

Edging

With WS together, join side of Front to one edge of first Side with a dc seam using A and 3.5mm (US size E/4) hook. Rep for second Side, then join Back in the same way. With WS together, attach Base to Front, Back and Sides in same way.
In Round 1, work into back loops only along dc of top edge.
ROUND 1 (RS): Using B and 3.5mm (US

Lining

From the lining fabric cut two pieces 28 x 24.5cm (11 x 9¾in) for front and back, two pieces 14 x 24.5cm (5½ x 9¾in) for sides, one piece 28 x 14cm (11 x 5½in) for base, and two pieces 6 x 30cm (2½ x 12in) for handles (or to fit measurements of crochet bag once made).

With RS together, pin and sew sides to front and back, taking a 1.5cm (5/8in) seam allowance throughout. Press seams open.

With RS together, pin and sew base to front, back and sides. Press seams open.

Fold 1.5cm (5/8in) to WS along top edge and press.

Fit lining inside crocheted bag and pin around top edge.

Handles:
Fold 1.5cm (5/8in) to WS along both long sides of the handles and press.

Pin lining onto WS of each crocheted handle. Hand sew lining onto each handle using whip stitch.

Insert one end of handle by about 1cm (3/8in) between lining and crochet piece positioned about 2.5cm (1in) from seam on front and the other end the same distance from the other seam, then pin in place. Repeat for other handle on back. Hand sew lining to top of crochet piece, securing the handles in place by stitching twice across the top of each end.

Finishing

Block, starch and press flowers. Sew one small flower at base of each handle end on front and back of bag.

Place one large flower on top of the other with petals alternating. Sew onto centre front of bag.

Rose Headband

This flower headband is a quick and easy project so is ideal for beginners. It can be made in a couple of hours and is perfect to keep your ears warm when you don't want to wear a hat.

MATERIALS
Debbie Bliss Cashmerino Aran (55% merino wool/33% microfibre/12% cashmere) Aran (worsted) yarn
- 1 x 50g (1¾oz) ball – approx 90m (98½yd) – of 027 Stone (**A**)

Rooster Almerino Aran (50% baby alpaca/50% merino wool) Aran (worsted) yarn
- 1 x 50g (1¾oz) ball – approx 94m (103yd) – of 313 Cherry (**B**)
- 5mm (US size H/8) crochet hook
- Yarn sewing needle

ABBREVIATIONS
ch	chain
dc	double crochet
htr	half treble
rep	repeat
RS	right side
sp(s)	space(s)
ss	slip stitch
st(s)	stitch(es)
tr	treble

SIZE
One size, but length is adjustable to fit any head size

MEASUREMENTS
49 x 9.5cm (19¼ x 3¾in)

TENSION
16 sts x 10 rows over a 10cm (4in) square working half treble using 5mm (US size H/8) hook.

Headband

Using A, make 15ch.
ROW 1: 1dc in 2nd ch from hook, 1dc in each ch to end. (14 sts)
ROW 2: 2ch, 1htr in each dc to end.
ROW 3: 2ch, 1htr in each htr to end.
ROW 4: 1ch, 1dc in each htr to end.
ROW 5: 1ch, 1dc in each dc to end.
Rep Rows 2–5 until work measures approx 49cm (19¼in) or to fit around head.
Fasten off.

Headband Gathering Strap

Using A, make 11ch.
ROW 1: 1htr in 3rd ch from hook, 1htr in each ch to end. (9 htr)
ROW 2: 2ch, 1htr in each htr to end.

Rep Row 2 six times more.
Fasten off.

Flower

Using B, make 55ch.
ROW 1 (RS): 1tr in 5th ch from hook, *1ch, miss 1 ch, [1tr, 1ch, 1tr] in next ch; rep from * to end of row.
ROW 2: 3ch, 5tr in first 1ch sp, *1dc in next 1ch sp, 6tr in next ch sp; rep from *, working last 6tr in last ch sp. (25 shells)
Fasten off, leaving a long tail for sewing flower together.

Finishing

Fold headband in half so short ends meet, with RS together.
Using A, join ends together with dc, working 1dc in each st through both layers.
Fasten off.
Turn RS out and sew in end.
Fold headband gathering strap around the headband so it covers the seam and join the ends together with dc as for the headband seam. Twist strap around so its seam is inside the headband.
To finish flower, thread needle with yarn tail and weave down side of shell to bottom. Roll first shell tightly to form centre bud. Make two stitches at base of shell to hold

Tip
Make the headband in a colour to match your outfit for an eye-catching effect.

bud in place and roll remaining strip around bud to form rose, securing as you roll by stitching through layers of chains at bottom of rose.
Sew rose in position onto headband gathering strap.

Baby Beanie Hat

The perfect gift for a christening or a first birthday, this beanie hat is easy to make and will keep a little one's head warm and cosy.

MATERIALS

Rooster Almerino Baby (50% baby alpaca/50% merino wool)
● 1 x 50g (1¾oz) ball – approx 125m (136½yd) – each of 501 Sea Spray (**A**), 503 Sandcastle (**B**), 504 Seaweed (**C**), 511 Anemone (**D**), 512 Horizon (**E**), 502 Seashell (**F**) and 507 Urchin (**G**)
● 3mm (US size D/3) crochet hook
● Yarn sewing needle

ABBREVIATIONS

ch	chain
cont	continu(e)(ing)
dc	double crochet
dtr	double treble
htr	half treble
rep	repeat
RS	right side
sp	space
ss	slip stitch
st(s)	stitch(es)
WS	wrong side

SIZE

Small: To fit age (approx) 3–12 months
Large: To fit age (approx) 1–2 years

MEASUREMENTS

Small: 35.5cm (14in) around, 11cm (4¼in) from crown to edge
Large: 40.5cm (16in) around, 12.5cm (5in) from crown to edge

TENSION

18 sts x 13 rows over a 10cm (4in) square working half treble using 3mm (US size D/3) hook.

Hat

Using A make 4ch, join with a ss in first ch to form a ring.
ROUND 1 (RS): 2ch (counts as first htr), 7htr in ring, join with a ss in first 2ch. (8 sts)
Cont in rounds with RS always facing.
ROUND 2: 2ch, 1htr at base of first 2ch, 2htr in each st to end, join with a ss in top of first 2ch. (16 sts)
ROUND 3: 2ch, 1htr at base of first 2ch, *1htr in next st, 2htr in next st; rep from * to last st, 1htr in last st, join with a ss in top of first 2ch. (24 sts)
ROUND 4: Rep Round 3. (36 sts)
ROUND 5: 2ch, 1htr at base of first 2ch, *1htr in each of next 2 sts, 2htr in next st; rep from * to last 2 sts, 1htr in each of last 2 sts, join with a ss in top of first 2ch. (48 sts)

Small size only:
ROUND 6: 2ch, 1htr at base of first 2ch, *1htr in each of next 7 sts, 2htr in next st; rep from * to last 7 sts, 1htr in each st to end, join with a ss in top of first 2ch. (54 sts)
ROUND 7: 2ch, 1htr at base of first 2ch, *1htr in each of next 8 sts, 2htr in next st; rep from * to last 8 sts, 1htr in each st to end, join with a ss in top of first 2ch. (60 sts)
ROUNDS 8-14: 2ch, 1htr in each st to end, join with a ss in first 2ch. (60 sts)
Fasten off A.
ROUND 15: Join B with a ss to any htr, 1ch, 1dc in each st to end, join with a ss in first dc.
ROUND 16: 1ch, 1dc in each st to end, join with a ss in first dc.
Fasten off.

Large size only:
ROUND 6: 2ch, 1htr at base of first 2ch, *1htr in each of next 3 sts, 2htr in next st; rep from * to last 3 sts, 1htr in each st to end, join with a ss in top of first 2ch. (60 sts)
ROUND 7: 2ch, 1htr at base of first 2ch, *1htr in each of next 5 sts, 2htr in next st; rep from * to last 5 sts, 1htr in each st to end, join with a ss in top of first 2ch. (70 sts)
ROUNDS 8-18: 2ch, 1htr in each st to end, join with a ss in top of first 2ch. (70 sts)
Fasten off A.
ROUND 19: Join B with a ss to any htr, 1ch, 1dc in each st to end, join with a ss in first dc.
ROUND 20: 1ch, 1dc in each st to end, join with a ss in first dc.
Fasten off.

Flowers

(MAKE 7 OR 8 USING ANY TWO OF B, C, D, E, F AND G FOR EACH)
Using first colour, 4ch, join with a ss in first ch to form a ring.
ROUND 1 (RS): 1ch, 5dc in ring, break off first colour, join second colour with a ss in first dc.
ROUND 2: *[4ch, 1dtr, 4ch, 1ss] in next st; rep from * 5 times more (6 petals), working last ss in dc at base of first 4ch.
Fasten off.
Sew in ends.

Finishing

Block and starch flowers.

Stalks:

Using same colour yarn as Round 1 of flower, join yarn with a ss in any two loops at back of flower (WS) near centre of Round 1.

Make between 4 and 6 chain for stalk (to make a variation on length of stalks), then with RS of hat facing, join flower with a ss in any two loops to centre of top of hat (attaching flowers around outside of Round 1).

Fasten off and sew in ends.

Attach all flowers in the same way.

MATERIALS

HAT
Rooster Almerino Aran (50% baby alpaca/50% merino wool) Aran (worsted) yarn
- 3 x 50g (1¾oz) balls – approx 282m (309yd) – of 315 Shimmer (**A**)
- 1 x 50g (1¾oz) ball – approx 94m (103yd) – of 318 Coral (**B**)

FLOWERS
Rooster Almerino DK (50% baby alpaca/50% merino wool) DK (light worsted) yarn
- Small amount of 210 Custard (**C**) and 201 Cornish (**D**)

- 3mm (US size D/3), 5mm (US size H/8) and 6mm (US size J/10) crochet hooks
- Yarn sewing needle

ABBREVIATIONS

ch	chain
cont	continu(e)(ing)
dc	double crochet
dtr	double treble
htr	half treble
rep	repeat
RS	right side
ss	slip stitch
st(s)	stitch(es)
yrh	yarn round hook

SPECIAL ABBREVIATIONS

htr2tog (half treble 2 stitches together) – [yrh, insert hook in next st, yrh, pull yarn through] twice, yrh, pull through all 5 loops on hook (one stitch decreased).

MEASUREMENTS

Small: 50cm (20in) circumference
Large: 54.5cm (21¾in) circumference

TENSION

11 sts x 9 rows over a 10cm (4in) square working half treble using 6mm (US size J/10) hook and two strands of A.

NOTES

Hat is made starting from top down and worked in a spiral. Mark the beginning and end of each round by inserting a stitch marker in loop on hook at the beginning of each round.

Ear Flap Hat

Look stylish while keeping your ears warm at the same time with this fashionable hat.

Hat

Use yarn double by using two balls of yarn, with one strand from each held together. Using A and 6mm (US size J/10) hook.
ROUND 1 (RS): 3ch (counts as first htr), 9htr in 3rd ch from hook. (10 sts) Cont in rounds with RS always facing.
ROUND 2: 2htr in top of 2ch at beg of Round 1, 2htr in each of next 9 htr. (20 sts)
ROUND 3: *1htr in next st, 2htr in next st; rep from * to end. (30 sts)
ROUND 4: *1htr in each of next 2 sts, 2htr in next st; rep from * to end. (40 sts)
ROUND 5: *1htr in each of next 3 sts, 2htr in next st; rep from * to end. (50 sts)
Small size only:
ROUND 6: *1htr in each of next 9 sts, 2htr in next st; rep from * to end. (55 sts)
ROUND 7: *1htr in each st to end.
ROUNDS 8–15: Rep Round 7.
Large size only:
ROUND 6: *1htr in each of next 4 sts, 2htr in next st; rep from * to end. (60 sts)

ROUND 7: *1htr in each st to end.
ROUNDS 8-17: Rep Round 7.
Both sizes:
Fasten off one strand only, do not break off second strand. Cont working with one strand of yarn only and using 5mm (US size H/8) hook.
First Ear Flap:
Put stitch marker in loop on hook.
*With RS facing, make 1htr in each of next 12 sts, turn.
NEXT ROW: 2ch, htr2tog over first two sts, 1htr in next 8 sts, htr2tog. (10 sts)
NEXT ROW: 2ch, htr2tog, 1htr in next 6 sts, htr2tog. (8 sts)
NEXT ROW: 2ch, htr2tog, 1htr in next 4 sts, htr2tog. (6 sts)
NEXT ROW: 2ch, htr2tog, 1htr in next 2 sts, htr2tog. (4 sts)
Fasten off.
Second Ear Flap:
With RS facing and using 5mm (US size H/8) hook and one strand of A only, fold hat flat and on opposite side to first flap, join yarn with a ss in st to correspond with last st of first row (of first flap), place marker in loop, 1ch; rep from * of First Ear Flap.
Edging:
ROUND I (RS): Using 5mm (US size H/8) hook and one strand of B, join yarn with a ss in first st of first flap, 1ch, 1dc in same place as ss, work a total of 20 dc evenly around flap (working 2dc in corners), 1dc in each st to next flap, work 20dc evenly around flap (working 2dc in corners), 1dc in each st to end, join with a ss in first dc.
Fasten off.

Flowers

(MakE 2)
Using 3mm (US size D/3) hook and C, make 4ch, join with a ss in first ch to form a ring.
ROUND I (RS): 1ch, 18dc in ring, break off C, join D with a ss in first dc. Cont with RS facing.
ROUND 2: [4ch, 1dtr in next st, 4ch, 1ss in next st] 9 times, working last ss at base of first 4ch. (9 petals)
Fasten off.

Finishing

Sew in ends on hat.
Close hole in centre of flowers by sewing around centre with tail of yarn C. Sew in ends to tidy up flower.
Block, starch and press flowers.
Arrange flowers on side at front of hat and sew in place.

MATERIALS

Rooster Almerino Aran (50% baby alpaca/50% merino wool) Aran (worsted) yarn
● 2 x 50g (1¾oz) balls – approx 188m (206yd) – 311 Deep Sea (**A**)
Debbie Bliss Angel (76% super kid mohair/24% silk) fine yarn
● Small amount of 31 Raspberry (**B**)
Rooster Delightful Lace (80% baby alpaca/20% silk) laceweight yarn
● Scrap of 601 Cusco (**C**)
● 2mm (US size B/1), 3.5mm (US size E/4) and 4.5mm (US size 7) crochet hooks
● Yarn sewing needle

ABBREVIATIONS

ch	chain
cont	continu(e)(ing)
dc	double crochet
htr	half treble
rep	repeat
RS	right side
ss	slip stitch
st(s)	stitch(es)
tr	treble
yrh	yarn round hook

SPECIAL ABBREVIATIONS

tr2tog (treble 2 stitches together) – [yrh, insert hook in next st, yrh, pull yarn through, yrh, pull through first 2 loops on hook] twice, yrh, pull through all 3 loops on hook (one stitch decreased).
htr2tog (half treble 2 stitches together) – [yrh, insert hook in next st, yrh, pull yarn through] twice, yrh, pull through all 5 loops on hook (one stitch decreased).

MEASUREMENTS

To fit an average-size woman's hand

TENSION

16 sts x 9 rows over a 10cm (4in) square working treble using 4.5mm (US size 7) hook and A.

NOTES

This pattern is made in the round, place a stitch marker in the beginning loop of each round, starting at Round 1.
There are also two different stitch markers for the thumb position on increasing rounds, use a contrasting colour for these markers.

Fingerless Gloves

These are lovely and simple and so desirable I have a line of people waiting for a pair! They are one size and made to fit an average sized woman, but if you want to make them bigger, try using smaller size hooks or a thinner wool such as double knit.

Glove

(MAKE 1 PAIR)
Starting at wrist end.
Using A and 4.5mm (US size 7) hook, make 32ch, join with a ss in first ch to form a ring. Place st marker (count marked st as last st) and change to 3.5mm (US size E/4) hook.
ROUND 1 (RS): 1tr in each ch to end. (32 sts)
Cont in rounds with RS always facing.
ROUND 2: Tr2tog, 1tr in each of next 14 sts, tr2tog, 1tr in each st to end. (30 sts)
ROUND 3: 1tr in each st to end. (30 sts)
ROUND 4: 1tr in each st to end.
ROUND 5: 1tr in each st to end.
ROUND 6: 1tr in each st to end.
ROUND 7: 1tr in each of next 12 sts, 2tr in next st (place thumb marker in first of these 2tr), 1tr in next st, 2tr in next st (place second thumb marker in last of these 2tr), 1tr in each st to end. (32 sts)
ROUND 8: 1tr in each st to end. (32 sts)
ROUND 9: 1tr in each st to first thumb marker, 2tr in next st – the one with thumb marker – (place thumb marker in first of these 2tr), 1tr in each st to next thumb marker, 2tr in next st – the one with thumb marker – (place second thumb marker in last of these 2tr), 1tr in each st to end of round. (34 sts)
ROUND 10: 1tr in each st to first thumb marker, 2tr in next st (place thumb marker in first of these 2tr), 1tr in

each st to next thumb marker, 2tr in next st (place second thumb marker in last of these 2tr), 1tr in each st to end. (36 sts)
ROUND 11: 1tr in each st to end. (36 sts)
ROUND 12: 1tr in each st to first thumb marker, 2tr in next st (place thumb marker in first of these 2tr), 1tr in each st to next thumb marker, 2tr in next st (place second thumb marker in last of these 2tr), 1tr in each st to end. (38 sts)
ROUND 13: 1tr in each st to end. (38 sts)
ROUND 14: 1tr in each st to first thumb marker, 2tr in next st (place thumb marker in first of these 2tr), 1tr in each st to next thumb marker, 2tr in next st (place second thumb marker in last of these 2tr), 1tr in each st to end. (40 sts)
ROUND 15: 1tr in each st to first thumb marker, miss 13 sts, 1tr in next st, 1tr in each st to end. (28 sts)
Remove thumb stitch markers only. Do not remove st marker to indicate beg of round.
ROUND 16: 1tr in each st to end. (27 sts)
ROUND 17: 1tr in each st to end. (27 sts)
ROUND 18: 1htr in each st to last 2 sts, htr2tog. (26 sts)
ROUND 19: 1dc in each st to last 2 sts, dc2tog. (25 sts)
ROUND 20: 1dc in each st to end, join with a ss in last st. (25 sts)
Fasten off.
Thumbhole:
With RS facing and using 3.5mm (US size E/4) hook, join A with a ss in first st of 13 sts missed for thumbhole in Round 15.
ROUND 1 (RS): 1ch, 1 dc in same place as last ss (place st marker), 1dc in each of next

12 sts around thumbhole. (13 dc)
Cont to work thumb in rounds with RS always facing.

ROUND 2: 1dc in first dc, 1dc in each each st to last 2 sts, dc2tog. (12 dc)

ROUND 3: 1dc in each st to end. (12 dc)

ROUND 4: 1dc in each st to last st, 1ss in last st.
Fasten off.

Edging:
With RS facing and using 3.5mm (US size E/4) hook, join A with a ss in underside of first chain at wrist end of glove.

ROUND I (RS): 1dc in each ch to end, join with a ss in first dc. (32 sts)
Cont with RS facing.

ROUND 2: 1ch, 1dc in same place as last ss, miss 1 st, 5tr in next st, miss 1 st, *1dc in next st, miss 1 st, 5tr in next st, miss 1 st; rep from * to end, join with a ss in first dc.
Fasten off.

Flowers

(MAKE 28)
Using B and 2mm (US size B/1) hook, make 4ch, join with a ss in first ch to form a ring.

ROUND I (RS): [3ch, 1ss in ring] 5 times, join with a ss in base of first 3ch.
Fasten off.
Sew around hole in centre to close.

Finishing

Sew in ends.
Turn glove inside out and hand sew gap at base of thumbhole to close it.
Using C, make a French knot in the centre of each flower.
With RS facing, sew 14 flowers evenly spaced around the wrist area of each glove.

Tip
Make sure you use stitch markers in different coloured strands of wool.

Bunting

Brighten up any room of the house with some traditional bunting! The flowers between the flags give it a wonderfully feminine feel.

MATERIALS

Rooster Almerino DK (50% baby alpaca/50% merino wool) DK (light worsted) yarn
- 1 x 50g (1¾oz) ball – approx 112.5m (123yd) – each of 211 Brighton Rock (**A**), 215 Lilac Sky (**B**), 216 Pier (**C**), 217 Beach (**D**), 218 Starfish (**E**) and 219 Sandcastle (**F**)
- 4mm (US size G/6) crochet hook
- Yarn sewing needle

MEASUREMENTS

111cm (43½in) long, excluding the ties

TENSION

Each flag measures 18.5cm (7¼in) along each side using a 4mm (US size G/6) hook.

ABBREVIATIONS

ch	chain
cont	continu(e)(ing)
dc	double crochet
rep	repeat
RS	right side
sp(s)	space(s)
ss	slip stitch
st(s)	stitch(es)
tr	treble

Flags

(MAKE 6, USING ANY THREE OF THE SIX COLOURS – A, B, C, D, E AND F – FOR EACH)

Using first colour, make 4ch, join with a ss in first ch to form a ring.

ROUND I (RS): 3ch (counts as 1tr), 3tr in ring, *[3ch, 4tr in ring] twice, 3ch, join with a ss in top of first 3ch.
Fasten off first colour.
Cont in rounds with RS always facing.

ROUND 2: Join second colour with a ss in any 3ch sp, 3ch (counts as 1tr), [4tr, 1ch, 5tr] in same sp, *1ch, [5tr, 1ch, 5tr] in next 3ch sp; rep from * once more, 1ch, join with a ss in top of first 3ch.
Fasten off second colour.

ROUND 3: Join third colour with a ss in 1ch sp between any two 5tr corner groups, 3ch (counts as 1 tr), [1tr, 2ch, 2tr] in same sp, *1tr in each of next 5 tr, miss 1ch sp, 1tr in each of next 5 tr, [2tr, 2ch, 2tr] in next 1ch sp (corner); rep from * once more, 1tr in each of next 5 tr, miss 1ch sp, 1tr in each of next 5 tr, join with a ss in top of first 3ch. Do not fasten off, but cont working with third colour to complete flag.

ROUND 4: 1ss in next tr, 1ss in next 2ch sp (corner), 3ch (counts as 1tr), [2tr, 3ch, 3tr] in same sp, *miss 1 tr, [3tr in next tr, miss 2 tr] 4 times, 3tr in next tr, [3tr, 3ch, 3tr] in next 2ch sp (corner); rep from * once more, miss 1 tr, [3tr in next tr, miss next 2 tr] 4 times, 3tr in next tr, join with a ss in top of first 3ch.

ROUND 5: 1ss in each of next 2 tr, 1ss in next 3ch sp (corner), 3ch (counts as 1tr), [2tr, 3ch, 3tr] in same sp, *3tr in each of next 6 sps between 3tr groups, [3tr, 3ch, 3tr] in next 3ch corner sp; rep from * once more, 3tr in each of next 6 sps between 3tr groups, join with a ss in top of first 3ch.

ROUND 6: 1ch, 1dc in same place as last ss, 1dc in each of next 2 tr, 3dc in next 3ch sp (corner), [1dc in each of next 24 tr, 3dc in next 3ch sp] twice, 1dc in each of next 21 tr, join with a ss in first dc, 1ss in each of next 2 dc.

Fasten off.

Top edge:

With RS of first flag facing and using A, join yarn with a ss in centre dc of any 3dc corner group of first flag, 1ch, 1dc in same place as ss, *1dc in each dc up to next 3dc corner group, 1dc in each of first 2 dc of group, take next flag and with RS facing, work 1dc in centre dc of any 3dc corner group (this joins flags together); rep from * until all flags are attached. Do not fasten off, but cont to work first tie as follows.

Ties

First tie:

Cont with A, make approx 59ch or until tie measures 30.5cm (12in) from edge of last flag.

Fasten off.

Second tie:

With RS facing, join A with a ss in top of first dc at start of top edge, make approx 59ch or until chain measures 30.5cm (12in) to match first tie.

Fasten off.

Flowers

(MAKE 7, USING ANY TWO OF THE SIX COLOURS – A, B, C, D, E AND F – FOR EACH)

Using first colour, make 6ch, join with a ss in first dc to form a ring.

ROUND 1: 1ch, 15dc in ring, enclosing yarn tail inside each dc around ring. Break off first colour, but do not fasten off.

ROUND 2: Join in second colour with 1ss in first dc in Round 1, *3ch, 1tr in each of next 2 dc, 3ch, 1ss in next dc st; rep from * 4 more times, working last ss in first dc. (5 petals) Fasten off.

Pull yarn tail to close up centre hole and sew in ends.

Finishing

Press and starch each flag. Sew on flowers along top of bunting – one between each pair of flags and one at each end.

Egg Cosies

Keep your breakfast eggs warm with these really cute cosies. They are very easy to make once you get the idea of crocheting in the spiral. Use a stitch marker to keep track of the beginning of each round – a scrap of a contrasting strand of yarn threaded through the stitch will do.

MATERIALS

EGG COSIES
Rooster Almerino DK (50% baby alpaca/50% merino wool) DK (light worsted) yarn
● Small amounts of 201 Cornish (**A**), 215 Lilac Sky (**B**), 218 Starfish (**C**), 211 Brighton Rock (**D**), 217 Beach (**E**) and 219 Sandcastle (**F**)

FLOWERS
Rooster Almerino Baby (50% baby alpaca/50% merino wool) yarn
● Scraps of 511 Anemone (**G**), 507 Urchin (**H**), 502 Seashell (**J**), 506 Bikini (**K**), 503 Sandcastle (**L**) and 510 Mermaid (**M**)
● 2mm (US size B/1) and 3.5mm (US size E/4) crochet hooks

ABBREVIATIONS

ch	chain
cont	continu(e)(ing)
dc	double crochet
rep	repeat
RS	right side
st(s)	stitch(es)
ss	slip stitch
tr	treble
WS	wrong side
yrh	yarn round hook

SPECIAL ABBREVIATION

dc2tog (double crochet 2 stitches together) – [insert hook in next st, yrh, pull yarn through] twice, yrh, pull through all 3 loops on hook (one stitch decreased).

MEASUREMENTS
Approx 4cm (1½in) diameter

TENSION
17 sts x 19 rows over a 10cm (4in) square working dc using 3.5mm (US size E/4) hook.

Cosy

(MAKE 1 EACH IN A, B, C, D, E AND F)
Using 3.5mm (US size E/4) hook, make 2ch, 6dc into 2nd ch from hook.
ROUND 1 (RS): 2dc in each dc to end. (12 dc)
Cont in rounds with RS always facing.
ROUND 2: Rep Round 1. (24 dc)
ROUNDS 3–7: 1dc in each dc to end.
ROUND 8: *1dc in next dc, dc2tog over next 2 dc; rep from * to end. (16 dc)
ROUND 9: 1dc in each dc, join with a ss in first dc of round.
Fasten off.

Flowers

(MAKE 1 EACH IN G, H, J, K, L AND M)
Using 2mm (US size B/1) hook, 4ch, join with a ss in first ch to form a ring.
ROUND 1 (RS): 1ch, 8dc in ring, join with a ss in first dc.
Cont with RS facing.
ROUND 2: *3ch, 1tr in same place as last ss, 1tr in next st, 3ch, 1ss in same place as last tr, 1ss in next st; rep from * to end, omitting last ss of last rep. (4 petals)
Fasten off.

Finishing

Sew in ends on the WS and turn cosy RS out. Using contrasting colour (G, H, J, K, L or M), make 5 or 6 bullion or French knots in centre of each flower. Sew one flower on top of each cosy.

MATERIALS

COVERS

Rooster Almerino DK (50% baby alpaca/50% merino wool) DK (light worsted) yarn
- 1 x 50g (1¾oz) ball – approx 112.5m (123yd) – each of 203 Strawberry Cream (**A**), 201 Cornish (**B**) and 216 Pier (**C**)

Rooster Almerino Baby (50% baby alpaca/50% merino wool) yarn
- 1 x 50g (1¾oz) ball – approx 125m (136½yd) – of 511 Anemone (**D**)

FLOWERS

Rooster Almerino Baby (50% baby alpaca/50% merino wool) yarn
- 1 x 50g (1¾oz) ball – approx 125m (136½yd) – of 506 Bikini (**E**), 502 Seashell (**F**) and 505 Candy Floss (**G**)

- 3mm (US size D/3) and 4mm (US size G/6) crochet hooks
- Sewing needle and matching thread
- 4 x elasticated bands
- 4 x 50cm (20in) lengths of narrow ribbon

ABBREVIATIONS

ch	chain
cont	continu(e)(ing)
htr	half treble
rep	repeat
RS	right side
ss	slip stitch
st(s)	stitch(es)
tr	treble

MEASUREMENTS

12–13cm (4¾–5in) in diameter

TENSION

Each cover in A, B and C measures 13cm (5in) in diameter and Cover in D measures 12cm (4¾in) in diameter, all using 4mm (US size G/6) hook.

Floral-edged Jam Pot Covers

These pot covers are irresistible and look simply fabulous on your kitchen shelf, or make wonderful gifts on top of homemade jam or chutney. They are made for standard 450g (1lb) jam jars; if you'd like them to be bigger, continue to increase after Round 5.

Cover

(MAKE 1 EACH IN A, B, C AND D)

Using 4mm (US size G/6) hook, 6ch, join with a ss in first ch to form a ring.

ROUND 1 (RS): 3ch (counts as first tr), 11tr in ring, join with a ss in top of first 3ch. (12 sts)

Cont in rounds with RS always facing.

ROUND 2: 3ch (counts as first tr), 1tr in same place as last ss, 2tr in each st to end, join with a ss in top of first 3ch. (24 sts)

ROUND 3: 3ch (counts as first tr), 1tr in same place as last ss, *1tr in next st, 2tr in each of next 2 sts; rep from * to last 2 sts, 1tr in next st, 2tr in last st, join with a ss in top of first 3ch. (40 sts)

ROUND 4: 3ch (counts as first tr) 1tr in same place as last ss, *1tr in each of next 3 sts, 2tr in next st; rep from * to last 3 sts, 1tr in each of last 3 sts, join with a ss in top of first 3ch. (50 sts)

ROUND 5: 3ch, 1tr in same place as last ss, *1tr in each of next 4 sts, 2tr in next st; rep from * to last 4 sts, 1tr into each of last 4 sts, join with a ss in top of first 3ch. (60 sts)

Fasten off.

Flowers

(MAKE 7 EACH IN D, E, F AND G)

Using 3mm (US size D/3) hook, 4ch, join with a ss in first ch to form a ring.

ROUND 1: [2ch, 1htr in ring, 2ch, 1ss in ring] 5 times.

Fasten off.

Sew centre to close.

Finishing

Sew seven flowers onto edge of each cover at approx 5cm (2in) intervals.

Embroider a French knot or bullion knot in the centre of each flower using a contrasting yarn colour.

Fit cover on top of jam pot and secure with an elasticated band. Tie ribbon around pot to decorate.

MATERIALS

PIN CUSHION 1

Rooster Almerino DK (50% baby alpaca/50% merino wool) DK (light worsted) yarn
- Small amounts of 201 Cornish (**A/B**), 205 Glace (**D/F**) and 207 Gooseberry (**E**)

Debbie Bliss Rialto DK (100% extra-fine merino wool) DK (light worsted) yarn
- Small amount of 42 Pink (**C**)

PIN CUSHION 2

Rooster Almerino DK (50% baby alpaca/50% merino wool) DK (light worsted) yarn
- Small amounts of 210 Custard (**A/C**), 205 Glace (**D**) and 208 Ocean (**F**)

Debbie Bliss Rialto DK (100% extra-fine merino wool) DK (light worsted) yarn
- Small amounts of 50 Deep Rose (**B**) and 42 Pink (**E**)

PIN CUSHION 3

Rooster Almerino DK (50% baby alpaca/50% merino wool) DK (light worsted) yarn
- Small amounts of 210 Custard (**A**), 217 Beach (**D/F**) and 205 Glace (**E**)

Debbie Bliss Rialto DK (100% extra-fine merino wool) DK (light worsted) yarn
- Small amounts of 42 Pink (**B**) and 50 Deep Rose (**C**)

- 4mm (US size G/6) crochet hook
- 2 x 12cm (4¾in) squares of thin cotton fabric or natural wadding and matching sewing thread
- Small amount of toy stuffing

ABBREVIATIONS

ch	chain
cont	continu(e)(ing)
dc	double crochet
htr	half treble
rep	repeat
RS	right side
sp(s)	space(s)
ss	slip stitch
st(s)	stitch(es)
tr	treble
WS	wrong side

SPECIAL ABBREVIATION

PC (popcorn) – work 5tr in next st, pull up the loop of 5th tr slightly and remove hook, then insert hook in top of first tr, reinsert hook in dropped loop of 5th tr (2 loops on hook), pull fifth tr through first tr and pull firmly.

MEASUREMENTS

Approx 11.5cm (4½in) square, including edging

TENSION

Front and back pieces (before edging is added) measure approx 7cm (2¾in) square using 4mm (US size G/6) hook.

Pin Cushions

These little pin cushions are just perfect for keeping pins and sewing needles safe. Choose colours from your stash as they use very little yarn. I use natural wadding for the lining instead of fabric, because this makes it easier to push in pins or wool sewing needles.

Front

Using A, make 4ch, join with a ss in first ch to form a ring.
ROUND 1 (RS): 1ch, 8dc in ring, break off A (see Tip), join B with a ss in first dc.
Cont in rounds with RS always facing.
ROUND 2: 3ch, 1PC in same dc as last ss, 2ch, [1PC in next dc, 2ch] 7 times, join with a ss in top of first PC. (8 petals)
Fasten off B.
ROUND 3: Join C with a ss in any 2ch sp, 3ch (counts as first tr), [2tr, 1ch, 3tr] in same sp, 1ch, 3tr in next 2ch sp, *1ch, [3tr, 1ch, 3tr] in next 2ch sp, 1ch, 3tr in next ch sp; rep from * twice more, 1ch, join with a ss in top of first 3ch.
Fasten off.

> **Tip**
> The pattern is for a two-colour flower; for a one-colour flower as on pin cushion 1, do not fasten off on Round 1 but continue to use A for Round 2.

Back

Using D, make 4ch, join with a ss to first ch to form a ring.
ROUND 1 (RS): 3ch, 2tr in ring, 2ch, [3tr in ring, 2ch] 3 times, join with a ss in top of first 3ch.
Cont in rounds with RS always facing.
ROUND 2: 1ss in each of next 2 tr, 1ss in next 2ch sp, 3ch, [2tr, 1ch, 3tr] in same sp, *1ch, [3tr, 1ch, 3tr] in next 2ch sp; rep from * twice more, 1ch, join with a ss in top of first 3ch.
ROUND 3: 1ss in each of next 2 tr, 1ss in next 1ch sp, 2ch (counts as first htr), [2htr, 1ch, 3htr] in same 1ch sp, 1ch, 3htr in next 1ch sp, 1ch, *[3htr, 1ch, 3htr] in next 1ch sp, 1ch, 3htr in next 1ch sp, 1ch; rep from * twice more, join with a ss in top of first 3ch.
Fasten off.

Finishing

Sew in ends.

Fabric pillow:

With WS together, sew two fabric squares together, taking a 1.5cm (5/8in) seam allowance and leaving small opening in one side. Turn RS out, fill very firmly with toy stuffing and sew opening closed.

Join Front and Back:

With front and back WS together, front facing upwards and working through both pieces, join E in any corner sp, 1ch, 2dc in same sp, *1dc in each st and ch sp to next corner, 2dc in corner; rep from * twice more, insert fabric pillow, 1dc in each st and ch sp to next corner (enclosing pillow), join with a ss in first dc.
Fasten off E.

Edging:

With front facing upwards, join F with a ss in 2nd st to right of any 2dc corner group, 5tr in 2nd dc of next 2dc corner group, *miss 1 dc, 1ss in next dc, [miss 1dc, 5tr in next dc, miss 1 dc, 1ss in next dc] twice, 5tr in 2nd dc of next 2dc corner group; rep from * twice, miss 1 dc, 1ss in next dc, [miss 1 dc, 5tr in next dc, miss 1 dc, 1ss in next dc] twice, working last ss in same place as first ss.
Fasten off.

Hexagon Flower Throw

This gorgeous throw looks complicated but actually involves simple techniques – it just takes a little time to complete, depending on how large you would like your throw to be.

MATERIALS

Rooster Almerino DK (50% baby alpaca/50% merino wool) DK (light worsted) yarn
- 15 x 50g (1¾oz) balls – approx 1687.5m (1845yd) – of 201 Cornish (**A**)
- 4 x 50g (1¾oz) balls – approx 450m (492yd) – each of 208 Ocean (**B**) and 205 Glace (**C**)
- 3 x 50g (1¾oz) balls – approx 337.5m (369yd) – each of 216 Pier (**D**), 218 Starfish (**E**) and 219 Sandcastle (**F**)
- 2 x 50g (1¾oz) balls – approx 225m (246yd) – each of 203 Strawberry Cream (**G**), 204 Grape (**H**), 215 Lilac Sky (**I**), 211 Brighton Rock (**J**) and 210 Custard (**K**)
- 1 x 50g (1¾oz) ball – approx 112.5m (123yd) – of 207 Gooseberry (**L**)
- 4mm (US size G/6) crochet hook

ABBREVIATIONS

ch	chain
Col	colour
cont	continu(e)(ing)
dc	double crochet
rep	repeat
RS	right side
sp(s)	space(s)
ss	slip stitch
st(s)	stitch(es)
tr	treble
yrh	yarn round hook

SPECIAL ABBREVIATION

1dc loop st (1 double crochet loop stitch) – insert hook in 1ch sp of round before previous round, yrh, pull yarn through drawing it up to extend the loop, yrh, pull yarn through both loops on hook to complete 1 double crochet loop stitch.

MEASUREMENTS

137 x 129.5cm (54 x 51in)

TENSION

Each hexagon measures approx 13cm (5in) from side to side and 15cm (6in) from point to point using 4mm (US size G/6) hook.

COLOUR COMBINATIONS

Make 17 each of hexagons 1–4, 16 of hexagon 5, 13 of hexagon 6, 6 of hexagon 7, 4 each of hexagons 8 & 9, 2 of hexagon 10, 1 of hexagon 11.

HEXAGON I: Col 1 = D, Col 2 = G, Col 3 = J, Col 4 = A

HEXAGON 2: Col 1 = E, Col 2 = I, Col 3 = H, Col 4 = A

HEXAGON 3: Col 1 = E, Col 2 = C, Col 3 = B, Col 4 = A

HEXAGON 4: Col 1 = B, Col 2 = F, Col 3 = K, Col 4 = A

HEXAGON 5: Col 1 = J, Col 2 = D, Col 3 = L, Col 4 = A

HEXAGON 6: Col 1 = F, Col 2 = C, Col 3 = B, Col 4 = A

HEXAGON 7: Col 1 = K, Col 2 = B, Col 3 = C, Col 4 = A

HEXAGON 8: Col 1 = E, Col 2 = H, Col 3 = I, Col 4 = A

HEXAGON 9: Col 1 = B, Col 2 = K, Col 3 = F, Col 4 = A

HEXAGON 10: Col 1 = E, Col 2 = B, Col 3 = C, Col 4 = A

HEXAGON II: Col 1 = G, Col 2 = L, Col 3 = D, Col 4 = A

Hexagon

(MAKE 114)

Using Col 1, make 5ch, join with a ss in first ch to form a ring.

ROUND 1 (RS): 3ch (counts as 1tr), 1tr in ring, 1ch, *2tr in ring, 1ch; rep from * 4 times more, join with a ss in top of first 3ch. (6 groups)

Fasten off Col 1.

Cont in rounds with RS always facing.

ROUND 2: Join Col 2 with a ss in any 1ch sp, 3ch, [1tr, 2ch, 2tr] in same sp, 1ch, *[2tr, 2ch, 2tr] in next 1ch sp, 1ch; rep from * 4 times more, join with a ss in top of first 3ch.

ROUND 3: 1ss in top of next tr, 1ss in next 2ch sp, 3ch, 6tr in same sp, 1ch, *7tr in next 2ch sp, 1ch; rep from * 4 times more, break off Col 3, but do not fasten off, join in Col 4 with a ss in top of first 3ch.

ROUND 4: 1ch, 1dc in same place as last ss, 1dc in each of next 6 tr, 1dc loop st in next 1ch sp of Round 2, *1dc in each of next 7 tr, 1dc loop st in next 1ch sp of Round 2; rep from * 4 times more, break off Col 3, but do not fasten off, join Col 4 with a ss in first dc.

ROUND 5: 3ch, 1tr in each of next 2 sts, 3tr in next st, 1tr in each of next 3 sts, *miss next dc loop st, 1tr in each of next 3 sts, 3tr in next st, 1tr in each of next 3 sts; rep from * 4 times more, join with a ss in top of first 3ch.

ROUND 6: 1ch, 1dc in same place as last ss, 1dc in each of next 3 tr, *3dc in next tr (centre st of 3tr group – corner), 1dc in each of next 8 tr; rep from * 4 times more, 3dc in next tr (centre tr of 3tr group – corner), 1dc in each of next 4 dc, join with a ss in first dc. Fasten off.

Finishing

Lay hexagons out on a flat surface to evenly arrange the colours. Using the diagram (below right) as an example, alternate hexagons in rows of 9 and then 10, starting the first row with 9 hexagons. Sew hexagons together with RS facing using whip stitch.

Edging:

With RS facing, join A with a ss in top right-hand corner hexagon, in any st along straight edge but not in any corner st (outer tip of hexagon), then work 1ch, 1dc in same place as ss, 1dc in each st to first outer tip (corner), 3dc in centre st of tip (centre st of a 3dc group), *1dc in each st to next corner outer tip, 3dc in centre st of next corner outer tip; rep from * to end, join with a ss in first dc. Fasten off.

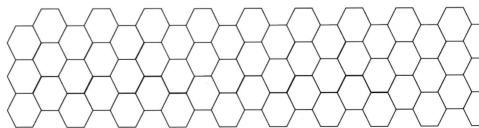

Chart for layout of hexagons

MATERIALS

Rooster Almerino DK (50% baby alpaca/50% merino wool) DK (light worsted) yarn
- 3 x 50g (1¾oz) balls – approx 337.5m (369yd) – of 201 Cornish (**A**)
- 1 x 50g (1¾oz) ball – approx 112.5m (123yd) – each of 220 Lighthouse (**B**), 217 Beach (**C**) and 211 Brighton Rock (**D**)

Rooster Almerino Baby (50% baby alpaca/50% merino wool)
- 1 x 50g (1¾oz) ball – approx 125m (136½yd) – of 511 Anemone (**E**)
- 3mm (US size D/3) crochet hook
- Toy stuffing
- 4 pairs of 9mm toy safety eyes
- Scraps of double-knitting-weight black yarn for embroidering nose, whiskers and mouth (**F**)

ABBREVIATIONS

ch	chain
cont	continu(e)(ing)
dc	double crochet
rep	repeat
RS	right side
ss	slip stitch
st(s)	stitch(es)
tr	treble
WS	wrong side
yrh	yarn round hook

SPECIAL ABBREVIATION

dc2tog (double crochet 2 stitches together) – [insert hook in next st, yrh, pull yarn through] twice, yrh, pull through all 3 loops on hook (one stitch decreased).

MEASUREMENTS

Cat: approx 18cm (7in) high
Kitten: approx 15cm (6in) high

TENSION

Approx 20 sts x 22 rows over a 10cm (4in) square working dc using a 3mm (US size D/3) hook.

NOTES

Each piece is worked in rounds in a spiral with RS always facing, except for neck shaping on body. Use a stitch marker in the first stitch of each round and count your stitches on **every** round.

Pansy and Kittens

This delightful cat and her three little kittens, Cocoa, Pebbles and Betty, make great gifts for children, who will treasure them for years.

PANSY

Head

Using A, make 2ch, 4dc in 2nd ch from hook.
ROUND 1 (RS): 2dc in each st to end. (8 sts)
ROUND 2: *1dc in next st, 2dc in next st; rep from * to end. (12 sts)
ROUND 3: *1dc in each of next 2 sts, 2dc in next st; rep from * to end. (16 sts)
ROUND 4: *1dc in each of next 3 sts, 2dc in next st; rep from * to end. (20 sts)
ROUND 5: *1dc in each of next 4 sts, 2dc in next st; rep from * to end. (24 sts)
ROUND 6: *1dc in each of next 5 sts, 2dc in next st; rep from * to end. (28 sts)
ROUND 7: *1dc in each of next 6 sts, 2dc in next st; rep from * to end. (32 sts)
ROUND 8: *1dc in each of next 7 sts, 2dc in next st; rep from * to end. (36 sts)
ROUND 9: [1dc in next st, 2dc in next st] 9 times, 1dc in each of next 18 sts. (45 sts)
ROUNDS 10-17: 1dc in each st to end. (45 sts)
ROUND 18: *1dc in each of next 7 sts, dc2tog; rep from * to end. (40 sts)
ROUND 19: *1dc in each of next 6 sts, dc2tog; rep from * to end. (35 sts)
ROUND 20: *1dc in each of next 5 sts, dc2tog; rep from * to end. (30 sts)
ROUND 21: *1dc in each of next 3 sts, dc2tog; rep from * to end. (24 sts)
ROUND 22: *1dc in each of next 2 sts, dc2tog; rep from * to end. (18 sts)
Insert eyes (between Rounds 10 and 11 and about 9 sts apart) and stuff head.
ROUND 23: *1dc in next st, dc2tog; rep from * to end. (12 sts)

ROUND 24: 1dc in each st to end. (12 sts)
Fasten off.

Body

Starting at bottom end.
Using A, make 2ch, 6dc in 2nd ch from hook.
ROUND 1 (RS): 2dc in each st to end. (12 sts)
ROUND 2: *1dc in next st, 2dc in next st; rep from * to end. (18 sts)
ROUND 3: *1dc in each of the next 2 sts, 2dc in next st; rep from * to end. (24 sts)
ROUND 4: *1dc in each of the next 3 sts, 2dc in next st; rep from * to end. (30 sts)
ROUNDS 5-15: 1dc in each st to end. (30 sts)
ROUND 16: *1dc in each of next 3 sts, dc2tog; rep from * to end. (24 sts)
ROUND 17: 1dc in each st to end, turn (leave stitch marker in st). (24 sts)

Neck:

ROW 18 (WS): Miss first st, 1dc in each of next 12 sts, turn (leaving rem 11 sts of round unworked).

ROW 19: Miss first st, 1dc in each of next 10 sts, turn (leaving remaining 11 sts of round unworked).

ROW 20: Miss first st, 1dc in each of next 8 sts, turn.

NEXT ROUND (RS): Miss first st, 1dc in each of next 7 sts, do not turn, work 2dc evenly down side of neck shaping, 1dc in next st (with stitch marker), 1dc in each of next 10 sts (rem sts left unworked in Row 18), work 3dc evenly up second side of neck shaping, join with a ss in first dc at start of round. (23 sts)

Fasten off, leaving a long enough yarn tail for sewing neck seam.

Ears

(MAKE 2)

Using A, make 2ch, 4dc in 2nd ch from hook.

ROUND 1 (RS): *2dc in next st, 1dc in next st; rep from * to end. (6 sts)

ROUND 2: *2dc in next st, 1dc in each of next 2 sts; rep from * to end. (8 sts)

ROUND 3: *2dc in next st, 1dc in each of next 3 sts; rep from * to end. (10 sts)

ROUND 4: *2dc in next st, 1dc in each of next 4 sts; rep from * to end. (12 sts)

ROUND 5: 1dc in each st to end. (12 sts)

ROUND 6: *2dc in next st, 1dc in each of next 5 sts; rep from * to end. (14 sts)

ROUND 7: *2dc in next st, 1dc in each of next 6 sts; rep from * to end. (16 sts)

Fasten off, leaving a long enough yarn tail for sewing ear to head.

Legs

(MAKE 4)

Using B, make 2ch, 6dc in 2nd ch from hook.

ROUND 1 (RS): 2dc in each st to end. (12 sts)

ROUND 2: *1dc in next st, 2dc in next st; rep from * to end. (18 sts)

ROUND 3: *1dc in each of next 2 sts, 2dc in next st; rep from * to end. (24 sts)

ROUNDS 4-6: 1dc in each st to end. (24 sts)

ROUND 7: [Dc2tog] 4 times, 1dc in each of next 16 sts. (20 sts)
Break off B, but do not fasten off.
ROUND 8: Join in A, 1dc in each st to end. (20 sts)
ROUND 9: *1dc in each of next 8 sts, dc2tog; rep from * to end. (18 sts)
Turn WS out and sew in ends, then turn RS out again to cont.
ROUND 10: 1dc in each st to end. (18 sts)
ROUND 11: *1dc in each of next 7 sts, dc2tog; rep from * to end. (16 sts)
ROUNDS 12–13: 1dc in each st to end. (16 sts)
ROUND 14: *1dc in each of next 6 sts, dc2tog; rep from * to end. (14 sts)
ROUNDS 15–16: 1dc in each st to end. (14 sts)
ROUND 17: *1dc in each of next 5 sts, dc2tog; rep from * to end. (12 sts)
ROUNDS 18–22: 1dc in each st to end. (12 sts)
Fasten off, leaving a long enough yarn tail for sewing leg to body.

Tail

Using B, make 2ch, 4dc in 2nd ch from hook.
ROUND 1 (RS): *1dc in next st, 2dc in next st; rep from * to end. (6 sts)
ROUND 2: *1dc in each of next 2 sts, 2dc in next st; rep from * to end. (8 sts)
ROUND 3: 1dc in each st to end. (8 sts)
ROUND 4: *1dc in each of next 3 sts, 2dc in next st; rep from * to end. (10 sts)
ROUNDS 5–7: 1dc in each st to end. (10 sts)
Break off B, but do not fasten off.
ROUND 8: Join in A, 1dc in each st to end. (10 sts)
ROUND 9: 1dc in each st to end. (10 sts)
ROUND 10: *1dc in each of next 3 sts, dc2tog; rep from * to end. (8 sts)
ROUNDS 11–16: 1dc in each st to end. (8 sts)
Fasten off, leaving a long enough yarn tail for sewing tail to body.

Flower

Using D, make 4ch, join with a ss in first ch to form a ring.

ROUND 1 (RS): [3ch, 1tr in ring, 3ch, 1ss in ring] 5 times.
Fasten off.

Finishing

Stuff body. Sew body to back of head with shaped neck extension in position at top (this makes head drop forwards).
Position ears on top of head about 2.5cm (1in) from neck seam and about 5 sts apart, pin in place and sew.
Stuff legs. Pin legs in position with longer end of toe facing the front, each pair 2–3 sts apart (the front pair two rounds from neck seam and back pair starting after Round 2). Make sure all the legs face downwards and are aligned with one another, then sew in place.
Pin and sew tail to top of body at end of cat, with contrasting tip pointing upwards.
Using F, embroider whiskers, mouth and nose.
Using E, make a French knot in centre of Flower and position in front of one ear, then pin and sew in place.
Collar:
Using C, make 28–30ch (test length around neck), 1ss in 2nd ch from hook, 1ss in each st to end. Fasten off.
Sew collar ends together around neck.

KITTENS
(MAKE 3)
Head

Using A, make 2ch, 4dc in 2nd ch from hook.
ROUND 1 (RS): 2dc in each st to end. (8 sts)
ROUND 2: *1dc in next st, 2dc in next st; rep from * to end. (12 sts)
ROUND 3: *1dc in each of next 2 sts, 2dc in next st; rep from * to end. (16 sts)
ROUND 4: *1dc in each of next 3 sts, 2dc in next st; rep from * to end. (20 sts)
ROUND 5: *1dc in each of next 4 sts, 2dc in next st; rep from * to end. (24 sts)
ROUND 6: *1dc in each of next 5 sts, 2dc in next st; rep from * to end. (28 sts)
ROUND 7: [1dc in next st, 2dc in next st] 7 times, 1dc in each of next 14 sts. (35 sts)
ROUNDS 8–11: 1dc in each st to end. (35 sts)
ROUND 13: *1dc in each of next 5 sts, dc2tog; rep from * to end. (30 sts)
ROUND 14: 1dc in each st to end. (30 sts)
ROUND 15: *1dc in each of next 4 sts, dc2tog; rep from * to end. (25 sts)
ROUND 16: *1dc in each of next 3 sts, dc2tog; rep from * to end. (20 sts)
Insert eyes (between Rounds 7 and 8 and 6–7 sts apart) and stuff head.
ROUND 17: *Dc2tog; rep from * to end. (10 sts)
ROUND 18: *Dc2tog; rep from * to end. (5 sts)
Fasten off.

Body

Starting at bottom end.
Using A, make 2ch, 6dc in 2nd ch from hook.
ROUND 1 (RS): 2dc in each st to end. (12 sts)
ROUND 2: *1dc in next st, 2dc in next st; rep from * to end. (18 sts)
ROUND 3: *1dc in each of the next 2 sts, 2dc in next st; rep from * to end. (24 sts)
ROUNDS 4–11: 1dc in each st to end. (24 sts)
ROUND 12: *1dc in each of next 2 sts, dc2tog; rep from * to end. (18 sts)
ROUND 13: 1dc in each st to end, turn (leave st marker in st).
Neck:
ROW 14 (WS): Miss first st, 1dc in each of next 9 sts, turn (leaving rem 8 sts in round unworked).
ROW 15: Miss first st, 1dc in each of next 7 sts, turn.
ROW 16: Miss first st, 1dc in each of next 5 sts, turn.
NEXT ROUND (RS): Miss first st, 1dc in each of next 4 sts, work 2dc evenly down side of neck shaping, 1dc in next st (with st marker), 1dc in each of next 7 dc (rem sts left unworked in Row 14), work 3dc up second side of neck shaping, join with a ss in first dc at start of round. (17 sts)
Fasten off, leaving a long enough yarn tail for sewing neck seam.

Ears

(MAKE 2 FOR EACH KITTEN)
Using A, make 4ch, 2dc in 2nd ch from hook.
ROUND 1 (RS): 2dc in each st to end. (8 sts)
ROUND 2: *1dc in each of next 3 sts, 2dc in next st; rep from * to end. (10 sts)
ROUND 3: *1dc in each of next 4 sts, 2dc in next st; rep from * to end. (12 sts)
ROUND 4: 1dc in each st to end.
Fasten off, leaving a long enough yarn tail for sewing ear to head.

Legs

(MAKE 4 FOR EACH KITTEN)
Using E, D or C, make 2ch, 6dc in 2nd ch from hook.
ROUND 1 (RS): 2dc in each st to end. (12 sts)
ROUND 2: *1dc in next st, 2dc in next st; rep from * to end. (18 sts)
ROUNDS 3-5: 1dc in each st to end. (18 sts)
Break off yarn, but do not fasten off.
ROUND 6: Join in A, [dc2tog] 4 times, 1dc in each of next 10 sts. (14 sts)
ROUND 7: *1dc in each of next 5 sts, dc2tog; rep from * to end. (12 sts)
ROUND 8: 1dc in each st to end. (12 sts)
Turn WS out and sew in ends, then turn RS out again to cont.
ROUND 9: *1dc in each of next 4 sts, dc2tog; rep from * to end. (10 sts)
ROUNDS 10-16: 1dc in each st to end. (10 sts)
Fasten off, leaving a long enough yarn tail for sewing leg to body.

Tail

Using E, D or C (same colour as used for paws), make 2ch, 4dc in 2nd ch from hook.
ROUND 1 (RS): *1dc in next st, 2dc in next st; rep from * to end. (6 sts)
ROUND 2: *1dc in each of next 2 sts, 2dc in next st; rep from * to end. (8 sts)
ROUND 3: 1dc in each st to end. (8 sts)
ROUND 4: *1dc in each of next 3 sts, 2dc in next st; rep from * to end. (10 sts)

Break off yarn, but do not fasten off.

ROUND 5: Join in A, 1dc in each st to end. (10 sts)

ROUNDS 6-9: 1dc in each st to end. (10 sts)

ROUND 10: *1dc in each of next 3 sts, dc2tog; rep from * to end. (8 sts)

ROUND 11: 1dc in each st to end. (8 sts) Fasten off, leaving a long enough yarn tail for sewing tail to body.

Flower

(MAKE I EACH IN D, B AND E)

Make 4ch, join with a ss in first ch to form a ring.

ROUND I (RS): [3ch, 1tr in ring, 3ch, 1ss in ring] 5 times.

Fasten off.

Finishing

Stuff each body. Sew body to back of each head with shaped neck extension in position at top (this makes head drop forwards). Position pair of ears on top of each head about 2.5cm (1in) from neck seam and about 3 sts apart, pin in place and sew.

Stuff legs. Pin legs in position with longer end of toe facing the front, each pair 2–3 sts apart (the front pair 1 round from neck seam and back pair starting after Round 2). Make sure all the legs face downwards and are aligned with one another, then sew in place. Pin and sew a tail to top of body at end of each kitten, with contrasting tip pointing upwards.

Using F, embroider whiskers, mouth and nose on each kitten.

To make tufts of hair, make small tassels on kitten's head and trim.

Using B, C or E, make a contrasting French knot in centre of each Flower. Sew a contrasting flower to each collar. (As an alternative to the flower in D, embroider a lazy daisy flower in D on top of the kitten's head and embroider a French knot in B in the centre of this flower.)

Collar:

Using B, D or E, make 23–25ch (test length around neck), 1ss in 2nd ch from hook, 1ss in each st to end. Fasten off.

Using a collar that contrasts with paws, sew collar ends together around neck.

Chapter 2
Practice Makes Perfect

If you're ready to make clusters and are confident changing colours, try some of these intermediate-level projects. Try the Shelf Edging (page 70), Place Mats (page 85), Oven Cloths (page 87) or Baby Blanket (page 97). You'll also find some beautiful flowers to make, which you can swap and change with other projects in the book.

Butterfly and Blossom Key Ring

The little flowers and butterfly make a very pretty addition to your key ring. They are made in cotton, which is more hard-wearing than yarn.

MATERIALS
Rowan Cotton Glacé (100% cotton)
- 1 x 50g (1¾oz) ball – approx 115m (125yd) – in each of 846 Cadmium (**A**), 850 Cobalt (**B**), 837 Baked Red (**C**), 725 Bubbles (**D**), 828 Heather (**E**), 845 Shell (**F**) and 814 Shoot (**G**)
- 3mm (US size D/3) crochet hook
- Sewing needle and matching thread
- Key ring

ABBREVIATIONS
ch	chain
cont	continu(e)(ing)
dc	double crochet
dtr	double treble
rep	repeat
RS	right side
ss	slip stitch
st(s)	stitch(es)
tr	treble
yrh	yarn round hook

MEASUREMENTS
Group of flowers and butterfly hang approx 5cm (2in) long from key ring

TENSION
Each flower measures approx 3cm (1¼in) in diameter and butterfly measures approx 3 x 3.5cm (1¼ x 1³/₈in) using 3mm (US size D/3) hook.

Butterfly Wings

Using A, make 11ch.
ROW 1 (RS): 2tr in 4th ch from hook, 2ch, 1dc in next ch, [1tr, 1dtr] in next ch, 3ch, 1ss in 3rd ch from hook (picot), 3ch, 1ss in next ch (first wing complete), 6ch, 1ss in 3rd ch from hook (picot), [1dtr, 1tr] in next ch, 2ch, 1dc in next ch, 2ch, 2tr in next ch, 2ch, 1ss in last ch.
Fasten off.
Sew wings together along centre (chain edge).

Butterfly Body

Using B, make 7ch.
ROW 1 (RS): 2dc in 2nd ch from hook, 1ss in each ch to end.
Fasten off.

Flowers

(MAKE 1 EACH IN D, E AND F)
Make 4ch, join with a ss in first ch to form a ring.
ROUND 1 (RS): [5ch, 1ss in ring] 5 times. (5 petals)
Fasten off.
Stalk:
Using G, join yarn with a ss in two loops at back of flower, make 6ch, break off G leaving approx 10cm (4in) tail.
Remove hook and set loop aside.
Rep on all flowers.

Finishing

Sew on body in centre of wings.

Using C, embroider a spot in each corner of wing.

To attach flowers, insert hook through smaller of rings on key ring (the larger is for the keys) and into loop of one flower stalk, yrh, pull yarn through loop and through ring. Fasten off.

Cont to attach each flower to ring.

To attach butterfly, using G, insert hook through ring (same place as flowers), join yarn with a ss in a loop at back of top of butterfly, yrh, pull yarn through loop on hook and through ring.

Fasten off.

Sew in each end along back of each ch of flower and of butterfly, securing butterfly and flowers with ends.

Tip
Use bright colours for this key ring to make your keys easier to find!

Blossom Necklace

This necklace is so pretty and can be made with any yarn, but don't use anything thicker than double knit. Always make the chain using a cotton yarn, as this does not stretch as much as some other fibres.

MATERIALS

LARGE BLOSSOMS
Rooster Almerino DK (50% baby alpaca/50% merino wool) DK (light worsted) yarn
● Small amount of 210 Custard (**A**)
Rooster Almerino Baby (50% baby alpaca/50% merino wool)
● Small amount of 502 Seashell (**B**)

SMALL BLOSSOMS
Rooster Almerino DK (50% baby alpaca/50% merino wool) DK (light worsted) yarn
● Small amounts each of 507 Urchin (**C**), 514 Lighthouse (**D**), 503 Sandcastle (**E**), 505 Candy Floss (**F**), 502 Seashell (**G**), 511 Anemone (**H**) and 509 Dolphin (**J**)

BASE CHAIN
Rowan Cotton Glacé (100% cotton)
● Small amount of 814 Shoot (**K**)

● 2.5mm (US size C/2) crochet hook
● Sewing needle and green thread

ABBREVIATIONS

ch	chain
cont	continu(e)(ing)
dc	double crochet
rep	repeat
RS	right side
ss	slip stitch
st(s)	stitch(es)
tr	treble
WS	wrong side

MEASUREMENTS

Approx 139cm (55in) long

TENSION

Large flower measures 4.5cm (1¾in) in diameter and small flower 2–2.5cm (¾–1in) in diameter using 2.5mm (US size C/2) hook.

Large Blossoms

(MAKE 3)
Using A, make 4ch, join with a ss in first ch to form a ring.
ROUND I (RS): 1ch, 10dc in ring, fasten off A, join B with a ss in first dc.
Cont with RS facing.
ROUND 2: *3ch, 3tr in next dc, 3ch, 1ss in next dc; rep from * working last ss at base of first 3ch. (5 petals)
Fasten off.

Small Blossoms

(MAKE 20: 2 IN C, 3 EACH IN D, E, F, G, H AND J)
Make 4ch, join with a ss in first ch to form a ring.
ROUND I (RS): [5ch, 1ss in ring] 5 times. (5 petals)
Fasten off.

Base Chain

Using K, make a chain measuring approx 139cm (55in), join with a ss in first ch to form a ring.
Fasten off and sew in ends.

Finishing

Pin one large blossom to the chain with WS of flower on RS of chain. Alternating colours, position six small blossoms and one large blossom on one side of the first large flower, then five small flowers and one large flower on the other side. Position the remaining nine small blossoms between the last two large blossoms. Pin the blossoms equally spaced apart around chain with WS of flowers on RS of chain.
Using sewing thread, sew flowers onto chain.

Flower Garland

I love this garland, especially in the kitchen to brighten up shelves. The bright colours will compliment any décor, but you could make them in pastel shades if you prefer.

MATERIALS

FLOWERS
Rooster Almerino DK (50% baby alpaca/50% merino wool) DK (light worsted) yarn
● 1 x 50g (1¾oz) ball – approx 112.5m (123yd) – each of 201 Cornish (**A**), 220 Lighthouse (**B**), 208 Ocean (**C**), 203 Strawberry Cream (**D**), 211 Brighton Rock (**E**), 217 Beach (**F**), 210 Custard (**G**) and 218 Starfish (**H**)
Rooster Almerino Baby (50% baby alpaca/50% merino wool)
● 1 x 50g (1¾oz) ball – approx 125m (137yd) – of 511 Anemone (**J**)

CHAIN
Rowan Cotton Glacé (100% cotton)
● 1 x 50g (1¾oz) ball – approx 115m (125yd) – of 814 Shoot (**K**)

● 3mm (US size D/3) crochet hook
● Yarn sewing needle

ABBREVIATIONS

ch	chain
cont	continu(e)(ing)
dc	double crochet
rep	repeat
RS	right side
ss	slip stitch
st(s)	stitch(es)
yrh	yarn round hook

MEASUREMENTS

71cm (28in) long, when stretched

TENSION

Each flower measures approx 8cm (3½in) in diameter using 3mm (US size D/3) hook and any colourway.

COLOUR COMBINATIONS

Make 1 of each colourway.
COLOURWAY 1: Col 1 = C, Col 2 = D, Col 3 = E
COLOURWAY 2: Col 1 = A, Col 2 = J, Col 3 = B
COLOURWAY 3: Col 1 = F, Col 2 = G, Col 3 = A
COLOURWAY 4: Col 1 = D, Col 2 = C, Col 3 = H
COLOURWAY 5: Col 1 = E, Col 2 = A, Col 3 = F
COLOURWAY 6: Col 1 = G, Col 2 = H, Col 3 = J
COLOURWAY 7: Col 1 = J, Col 2 = B, Col 3 = D
COLOURWAY 8: Col 1 = B, Col 2 = E, Col 3 = A

Flower

(MAKE 8)
Using Col 1, 4ch, join with a ss in first ch to form a ring.
ROUND 1 (RS): 1ch, 8dc in ring, join with a ss in first dc. (8 sts)
Cont in rounds with RS always facing.
ROUND 2: 1ch, 2dc in same st as ss, [1dc in next st, 2dc in next st] 3 times, 1dc in next st, break off Col 1, join in Col 2 with a ss in front loop only of first dc. (12 sts)
ROUND 3: Working in front loops only, [4ch, 1ss in next st] 12 times. (12 loops)
Fasten off.
ROUND 4: Working in back loops only, join Col 3 with a ss back loop of first dc of Round 2, 1dc in same place as ss, [10ch, 1dc in back loop of next st] 12 times, join with a ss in first dc. (12 loops)
Fasten off.

Finishing

Block and starch outer petals of all flowers. Using K, make a chain of approx 10cm (4in), * with RS facing, insert hook in any petal loop of flower, yrh, pull yarn through petal loop and loop on hook, 10ch; rep from * until all flowers are attached, cont chain at end to approx 10cm (4in) to match first end chain.
Fasten off.
Sew in ends.

MATERIALS

Rowan Cotton Glacé (100% cotton)
- 1 x 50g (1¾oz) ball – approx 115m (125yd) –
each of 829 Twilight (**A**), 827 Chalk (**B**),
832 Persimmon (**C**) and 725 Ecru (**D**)
- 3mm (US size D/3) crochet hook
- Sewing needle and matching thread

ABBREVIATIONS

beg	beginning
ch	chain
cont	continu(e)(ing)
dc	double crochet
dtr	double treble
htr	half treble
sp	space
ss	slip stitch
tr	treble
rep	repeat
RS	right side
st(s)	stitch(es)
yrh	yarn round hook

SPECIAL ABBREVIATION

dtrCLV (double treble cluster V) – yrh twice, insert
hook in same st as last dtr (or tr) made, pull yarn
through, yrh, pull through first 2 loops on hook, yrh
twice, miss 2 sts, insert hook in next st, pull yarn
through, yrh, pull through first 2 loops on hook,
yrh, pull yarn through all 5 loops on hook.

MEASUREMENTS

Make to size – sample measures 98cm (38½in) long
by 13cm (5in) deep

TENSION

Edging is 5cm (2in) wide and has 7 V-stitches to
10cm (4in), Flower is 8cm (3⅛in) in diameter,
Leaves are 4cm (1½in) long – all using 3mm (US
size D/3) hook.

NOTE

Measure your shelf edge and make enough chain to
fit the measurement. Allow for multiples of 3 chain
plus 1 for the base chain.

Shelf Edging

This is such an attractive idea to decorate a plain and
boring shelf. I use this edging underneath my television
to cover up the DVD player beneath, but this kind of
shelf edge looks great anywhere.

Edging

Using A, make 208ch.
ROW 1: 1dc in 2nd ch from hook, 1dc in
each ch to end. (207 dc)
ROW 2: 4ch, miss first st, 1dtr in next st,
2ch, *1dtrCLV, 2ch; rep from * to last st,
1tr in last st.
ROW 3: 4ch, 1dtrCLV in top of first tr and
next dtrCLV, *2ch, 1dtrCLV in top of last
dtrCLV and next dtrCLV; rep from * to
end, working last leg of last dtrCLV in next
dtr, 2ch, 1tr in top of 4ch.
ROW 4: 4ch, 1dtr in top of first dtrCLV,
*2ch, 1dtrCLV in top of last dtrCLV and
next dtrCLV; rep from * to end, 2ch, 1tr in
top of 4ch.
ROW 5: 1ch, 1dc in first tr, *2dc in next
ch sp, 1dc in top of next dtrCLV; rep from
* to last ch sp, 2dc in last ch sp, 1dc in top
of 4ch.
Fasten off.

Flowers

(MAKE 7 OR AS REQUIRED)
Using B, make 6ch, join with a ss in first ch
to form a ring.
ROUND 1 (RS): 1ch, 10htr in ring, break
off B, join in C with a ss in first htr. (10 sts)
Cont in rounds with RS always facing.
ROUND 2: 1ch, 2dc in each st to end,
break off C, join in D with a ss in first dc.
(20 sts)

Petals:
ROW 3: Using D, 3ch, 2tr in each of next
3 dc, turn.
ROW 4: 1ch, miss first st, 1dc in each of
next 5 tr, turn.
ROW 5: 3ch, miss first st, 1ss in next st,
[3ch, 1ss in next st] 3 times, 3ch, 1ss in 1ch at
end, 3ch, 1ss in next dc of Round 2.
Rep Rows 3–5 until 5 petals are made,
working last ss of last petal at base of first
3ch of Row 3 of first petal.
Fasten off.

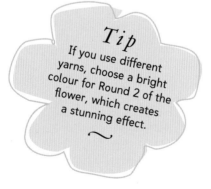

Tip
If you use different
yarns, choose a bright
colour for Round 2 of the
flower, which creates
a stunning effect.

Leaves

(MAKE 14 OR AS REQUIRED)
Using B, make 8ch.
ROUND I (RS): 1ss in 2nd ch from hook,
1dc in next ch, 1htr in next ch, 1tr in next ch,
1htr in next ch, 1dc in next ch, 1ss in next ch,
1ch, turn work so bottom of foundation chain
is at top and cont along bottom of sts just
made, 1ss in first ch, 1dc in next ch, 1htr in
next ch, 1tr in next ch, 1htr in next ch, 1dc in
next ch, 1ss in next ch, 1ss in tip of leaf.
Fasten off.

Finishing

Sew in ends.
Block and press all flowers and leaves.
Pin flowers in place evenly along main piece,
with flowers about 5–6.5cm (2–2½in) apart
and with first and last flowers about 2.5cm
(1in) from end of main piece. Pin leaves in
place starting with one leaf at the ends and
with two leaves between flowers.
Sew on flowers by stitching top edge of one
petal of flower to main piece with RS of main
piece and RS of flower facing. Sew tips of
leaves to main piece and sew to each flower
on a side petal.

Floral Shell Stitch Cushion Cover

Made using an easy shell stitch and decorated with a bouquet of flowers in the middle, this is a great project for beginners/intermediate. I used scraps of different reds for the roses, as well as pinks and yellow, but use up any colours in your stash.

Front and Back

(MAKE 2 THE SAME)
Using MC and 5mm (US size H/8) hook, make 62ch.

ROW I (RS): 1dc in 2nd ch from hook, *miss 2 ch, 5tr in next ch, miss 2 ch, 1dc in next ch; rep from * to end.
ROW 2: 3ch, 2tr in first dc, *miss 2 tr, 1dc in next tr, miss 2 tr, 5tr in next dc; rep from

---

MATERIALS

CUSHION
Rooster Almerino Aran (50% baby alpaca/50% merino wool) Aran (worsted) yarn
● 6 x 50g (1¾oz) balls – approx 564m (618yd) – of 315 Shimmer (**MC**)

OPEN ROSES
Rooster Almerino Aran (50% baby alpaca/50% merino wool) Aran (worsted) yarn
● 1 x 50g (1¾oz) ball – approx 94m (103yd) – of 310 Rooster (**A**)
Rooster Almerino DK (50% baby alpaca/50% merino wool) DK (light worsted) yarn
● Small amount of 220 Lighthouse (**B**)
Debbie Bliss Cashmerino DK (55% merino wool/33% microfibre/12% cashmere) DK (light worsted) yarn
● Small amount of 42 Rose Pink (**C**)
Cascade 220 (100% Peruvian highland wool) Aran (worsted) yarn
● Small amount of 8414 Bright Red (**D**)

CLOSED ROSE
Debbie Bliss Cashmerino Aran (55% merino wool/33% microfibre/12% cashmere) Aran (worsted) yarn
● Small amount of 49 Coral (**E**)

SMALL BLOSSOM FLOWERS
Rooster Almerino Baby (50% baby alpaca/50% merino wool)
● Small amount of 503 Sandcastle (**F**)

LEAVES
Rooster Almerino DK (50% baby alpaca/50% merino wool) DK (light worsted) yarn
● Small amount of 207 Gooseberry (**G**)

● 3mm (US size D/3), 4mm (US size G/6) and 5mm (US size H/8) crochet hooks
● 45cm (18in) square cushion pad
● Yarn sewing needle

ABBREVIATIONS

ch	chain
cont	continu(e)(ing)
dc	double crochet
dtr	double treble
rep	repeat
RS	right side
sp(s)	space(s)
ss	slip stitch
st(s)	stitch(es)
tr	treble
WS	wrong side

MEASUREMENTS
To fit a 45cm (18in) square cushion pad

TENSION
13 sts x 8 rows over a 10cm (4in) square working Shell Stitch using 5mm (US size H/8) hook.

* ending last rep with 3tr (instead of 5tr) in last dc.

ROW 3: 1ch, 1dc in first tr, *miss 2 tr, 5tr in next dc, miss 2 tr, 1dc in next tr; rep from * working last dc of last rep in top of 3ch.
Rep Rows 2 and 3 until work measures 45cm (18in), ending on a Row 3.
Fasten off.

Edging

Using MC and 5mm (US size H/8) hook and with RS facing, join MC with a ss in one corner, 1ch, work 61 dc evenly along each edge of Front, working 2 dc in each corner, join with a ss in first dc.
Fasten off.
Rep for Back.

Join Front and Back:
With Front and Back WS together and working each st through both layers, join A with a ss in any st along one edge, 1ch, 1dc in same place as ss, 1dc in each st around 3 sides of cushion, working 2dc in each corner st, then insert cushion pad, cont along last side to close cover, join with a ss in first dc.
Fasten off.

Shell edging:
Join MC with a ss in 2nd st of first corner, 1ch, 1dc in same place as ss, *miss 1 st, 5tr in next st, miss 1 st, 1dc in next st; rep from * to end omitting dc at end of last rep, join with a ss in first dc.
Fasten off.

Large Open Rose

(MAKE 1 EACH IN A, B AND C)
Using A and 5mm (US size H/8) hook, 5ch, join with a ss in first ch to form a ring.
ROUND 1 (RS): [1dc, 1tr, 1dc] 4 times in ring. (4 petals)

Cont in rounds with RS always facing.
ROUND 2: Keeping ch loops behind petals and bending petals forwards to work into back of petals, [2ch, from WS 1ss in 2 loops at base of 2nd dc of next petal] 4 times. (4 loops)
ROUND 3: [4tr in next 2ch sp (loop just made in Round 2), 1ss in same ch sp] 4 times. (4 petals)
ROUND 4: Using same colour and bending petals forwards to work into back of petals, join yarn from WS with a ss in 2 loops at base of highest point of any petal, [3ch, 1ss in 2 loops at base of highest point of next petal] 4 times, working last ss in first ss. (4 loops)
ROUND 5: [8tr in next ch sp, 1ss in same ch sp] 4 times, working last ss in base of first tr. (4 petals)
Fasten off.
Using 4mm (US size G/6) hook, make one Large Open Rose in B and one in C.

Small Open Rose

(MAKE 1)
Using D and 5mm (US size H/8) hook, work as for Large Open Rose to end of Round 3.
Fasten off.

Closed Rose

(MAKE 1)
Using E and 4mm (US size G/6) hook, make 48ch.
Work all petals along 53ch with RS facing as follows.
PETALS 1–3: Miss 3 ch, 1tr in each of next 2 ch, 2ch, 1ss in next ch, *3ch, 1tr in each of next 2 ch, 2ch, 1ss in next ch; rep from * once more. (3 petals)
PETALS 4–6: *4ch, 1dtr in each of next 4 ch, 3ch, 1ss in next ch; rep from * twice more.
PETALS 7–9: *4ch, 1dtr in each of next 6 ch, 3ch, 1ss in next ch; rep from * twice more.
Fasten off.
With WS facing and starting with smaller petals, coil petals of closed rose keeping base flat at chain edge, then stitch in place at base, ensuring that all petals are secure.

Small Blossom Flowers

(MAKE 2)
Using F and 3mm (US size D/3) hook, make 4ch, join with a ss in first ch to form a ring.
ROUND 1 (RS): [5ch, 1ss in ring] 5 times. (5 petals)
Fasten off.
Weave end around centre, pull to close hole and secure.

Leaves

(MAKE 3)
Using G and 4mm (US size G/6) hook, make 8ch.
ROUND 1 (RS): 1dc in 2nd ch from hook, 1htr in next ch, 1tr in each of next 2 ch, 2tr in next ch, 1htr in next ch, 1dc in next ch, 2ch, turn work so bottom of foundation ch is at top and cont along bottom of sts just make, 1dc in first ch, 1htr in next ch, 2tr in next ch, 1tr in each of next 2 ch, 1htr in next ch, 1dc in last ch, join with a ss in tip of leaf.
Fasten off.

Finishing

Sew in ends.
Arrange flowers and leaves on centre of cushion front, pin and sew in place.

Tablecloth

Great for both indoor and outdoor use, this pretty tablecloth works really well when made using double knitting-weight cotton.

MATERIALS
Debbie Bliss Cotton DK (100% cotton) DK/Aran (worsted) yarn
● 17 x 50g (1¾oz) balls – approx 1428m (1564yd) – of 61 Aqua (**A**)
DMC Natura Just Cotton (100% cotton) 4ply (fingering) yarn
● 1 x 50g (1¾oz) ball – approx 155m (170yd) – of N16 Tournesol (**B**)
● 4.5mm (US size 7) and 7mm (US size K10½) crochet hooks
● Yarn sewing needle

ABBREVIATIONS
ch	chain
cont	continu(e)(ing)
dc	double crochet
rep	repeat
RS	right side
ss	slip stitch
st(s)	stitch(es)
tr	treble

MEASUREMENTS
Approx 102cm (40in) square

TENSION
[1tr, 1 shell group] twice x 6 rows over a 10cm (4in) square working shell pattern using 7mm (US size K10½) hook and A.

Tablecloth

Using A and 7mm (US size K10½) hook, make 122ch.

ROW 1: 1dc in 2nd ch from hook, *miss 2 ch, 5tr in next ch (shell made), miss 2 ch, 1tr in next ch; rep from * ending with 1dc (instead of tr) in last ch.

ROW 2: 3ch, 2tr in first st (half shell), *1tr in centre tr of next shell, miss next 2 tr (remainder of shell)**, 5tr in next tr (between shells); rep from * ending last rep at **, 3tr in last st.

ROW 3: 1ch, 1tr in first tr, miss 2 tr, *5tr in next tr**, 1tr in centre tr of next shell; rep from * ending last rep at **, 1tr in top of 3ch. Rep Rows 2 and 3 until a total of 61 rows have been worked.
Fasten off.

Edging

With RS facing and 7mm (US size K10½) hook, join A in any corner st, 3ch, 4tr in same st, miss 2 sts (or equivalent), 1tr in next st, miss 2 sts, *5tr in next st, miss 2 sts, 1tr in next st, miss 2 sts; rep from * evenly all around edge of tablecloth (working a 5tr group in each corner), join with a ss in top of first 3ch.
Fasten off.

Flowers

(MAKE 4)
Using B and 4.5mm (US size 7) hook, make 4ch.

ROW 1: Miss first 2 ch, 1dc in each of next 2 ch, 17ch.

ROW 2: Miss 17 ch, 1dc in each of next 2 dc, 1dc in top of first 2ch.

ROW 3: 1ch, miss 1 dc, 1dc in each of next 2 dc, 17ch.

ROW 4: Miss 17 ch, 1dc in each of next 2 dc, 1dc in top of first 1ch.
[Rep Rows 3 and 4] 34 times more.
Fasten off, leaving a long tail for sewing flower together.

Finishing

Sew in ends on tablecloth.
Coil the straight edge (base of flower) and stitch across the base to secure in place. Using a wool sewing needle and with RS facing, catch a loop between any two 17-ch groups on the second coiled row in from the back, and sew a flower onto each corner of tablecloth.

Lido Swimming Cap Tea Cosy

This fun tea cosy reminds me of a swimming cap my mum used to wear in the 1950s! Teapots come in all different shapes and sizes. This tea cosy pattern is based on an average size teapot to serve about 4 to 6 cups.

Cosy

(MAKE 2 SIDES)

Use yarn double throughout by winding main ball into two smaller balls and using 2 strands together.

Using A double and 6mm (US size J/10) hook, make 29ch.

ROW 1: 1dc in 2nd ch from hook, 1dc in each ch to end. (28 dc)

ROW 2: 1ch, 1dc in each dc to end.

Rep Row 2 until work measures 8cm (3in).

NEXT ROW: 1ch, dc2tog, 1dc in each st to last 2 sts, dc2tog. (26 dc)

NEXT ROW: 1ch, 1dc in each st to end.

NEXT ROW: 1ch, dc2tog, 1dc in each st to last 2 sts, dc2tog. (24 dc)

NEXT ROW: 1ch, 1dc in each st to end.

NEXT ROW: 1ch, dc2tog, 1dc in each st to last 2 sts, dc2tog. (22 dc)

NEXT ROW: 1ch, 1dc in each st to end.

NEXT ROW: 1ch, dc2tog, 1dc in each st to last 2 sts, dc2tog. (20 dc)

NEXT ROW: 1ch, 1dc in each st to end.

NEXT ROW: 1ch, dc2tog, 1dc in each st to

last 2 sts, dc2tog. (18 dc)

Rep last row until 8 sts remain.

NEXT ROW: [Dc2tog] 4 times. (4 dc)

NEXT ROW: [Dc2tog] twice. (2 dc)

Fasten off.

MATERIALS

COSY

Rooster Almerino Aran (50% baby alpaca/50% merino wool) Aran (worsted) yarn

● 4 x 50g (1¾oz) balls – approx 376m (412yd) – of 301 Cornish (**A**)

FLOWERS

Debbie Bliss Cashmerino Aran (50% merino wool/33% microfibre/12% cashmere) Aran (worsted) yarn

● 1 x 50g (1¾oz) ball – approx 90m (98½yd) – of 300 Black (**B**)

Rooster Almerino DK (50% baby alpaca/50% merino wool) DK (light worsted) yarn

● 1 x 50g (1¾oz) ball – approx 112.5m (123yd) – each of 201 Cornish (**C**), 220 Lighthouse (**D**), 215 Lilac Sky (**E**), 211 Brighton Rock (**F**) and 210 Custard (**G**)

● 6mm (US size J/10) and 3.5mm (US size E/4) crochet hooks

● Yarn sewing needle

ABBREVIATIONS

ch	chain
cont	continu(e)(ing)
dc	double crochet
rep	repeat
RS	right side
ss	slip stitch
st(s)	stitch(es)
tr	treble
WS	wrong side
yrh	yarn round hook

SPECIAL ABBREVIATION

dc2tog (double crochet 2 stitches together) – [insert hook in next st, yrh, pull yarn through] twice, yrh, pull through all 3 loops on hook (one stitch decreased).

MEASUREMENTS

To fit a medium-size teapot (4–6 cups)

TENSION

11 sts x 15 rows over a 10cm (4in) square working dc using 6mm (US size J/10) hook and 2 strands of A.

COLOUR COMBINATIONS

Make 11 of Colourway 1, 12 of Colourway 2, 13 of Colourway 3, 12 of Colourway 4.

COLOURWAY 1: Col 1 = B, Col 2 = C, Col 3 = D
COLOURWAY 2: Col 1 = B, Col 2 = C, Col 3 = E
COLOURWAY 3: Col 1 = B, Col 2 = C, Col 3 = F
COLOURWAY 4: Col 1 = B, Col 2 = C, Col 3 = G

Flower

(MAKE 48)

Using Col 1 and 3.5mm (US size E/4) hook, 4ch, join with a ss in first ch to form a ring.

ROUND 1 (RS): 1ch, 6dc in ring, break off Col 1, join in Col 2 with a ss in first dc. (6 dc)
Cont in rounds with RS always facing.

ROUND 2: 1ch, 2dc in same place as last ss, *2dc in next dc; rep from * to end, break off Col 2, join in Col 3 with a ss in first dc. (12 dc)

ROUND 3: *3ch, 2tr in next dc, 3ch, 1ss in next dc; rep from * to end, working last ss at base of first 3ch. (6 petals)
Fasten off.

Finishing

Pin cosy sides WS together, leaving an opening on each side for handle and spout – try on teapot and pin to fit, or pin and sew 2.5cm (1in) at bottom of each side, leave a 10cm (4in) opening on each side, then sew seam across top and down sides. Turn RS out.

Pin one of each colour flower tightly together around top. Pin other flowers, with colours evenly spaced, all around cosy using large glass-headed pins. Sew in place.

MATERIALS

Rooster Almerino DK (50% baby alpaca/50% merino wool) DK (light worsted) yarn
- 2 x 50g (1¾oz) balls – approx 225m (246yd) – each of 211 Brighton Rock (**A**) and 214 Damson (**E**)
- 1 x 50g (1¾oz) ball – approx 112.5m (123yd) – each of 216 Pier (**B**), 201 Cornish (**C**) and 218 Starfish (**D**)
- 3 x 50g (1¾oz) balls – approx 337.5m (369yd) – of 215 Lilac Sky (**F**)
- 4mm (US size G/6) crochet hook
- 40cm (16in) square cushion pad

ABBREVIATIONS

ch	chain
cont	continu(e)(ing)
dc	double crochet
rep	repeat
RS	right side
sp(s)	space(s)
ss	slip stitch
st(s)	stitch(es)
tr	treble
WS	wrong side
yrh	yarn round hook

SPECIAL ABBREVIATION

2trCL picot (2 treble cluster picot) – [yrh, insert hook in st (or sp), yrh, pull yarn through, yrh, pull yarn through first 2 loops on hook] twice in same st (or sp), yrh, pull yarn through all 3 loops on hook, 3ch, insert hook from right to left through the top 3 loops of 2trCL just made (4 loops on hook), yrh, pull yarn through all 4 loops on hook.

MEASUREMENTS

To fit a 40cm (16in) square cushion pad

TENSION

13 sts (approx 4½ 3tr shells) x 7 rows over a 10cm (4in) square working shell pattern using 4mm (US size G/6) hook.

Crown-edged Cushion Cover

This is one of the easiest projects in this book, but I just love this traditional square using more contemporary colours.

Front

(MAKE 1)
Using A, 4ch, join with a ss in first ch to form a ring.
ROUND 1 (RS): 3ch (counts as first tr), 2tr in ring, 2ch, *3tr in ring, 2ch; rep from * twice more, join with a ss in top of first 3ch.

Fasten off A.
Cont in rounds with RS always facing.
ROUND 2: Join B with a ss in any 2ch sp, 3ch, 4tr in same sp, 1tr in centre st of next 3tr group, *5tr in next 2ch sp, 1tr in centre st of next 3tr group; rep from * twice more, join with a ss in top of first 3ch.
Fasten off B.

sp between 3rd and 4th tr of next 6tr group, 3tr in each sp to next 6tr corner group; rep from * twice more, join with a ss in top of first 3ch.

ROUNDS 7-17: [Rep Round 6] 11 times (increasing the number of 3tr groups between corners in each round) – work now measures approx 40cm (16in) square.
Fasten off.

Back

(MAKE 1)
Using F, make 4ch, join with a ss in first ch to form a ring.
ROUND 1 (RS): As Round 1 of front.
Cont in rounds with RS always facing.
ROUND 2: 1ss in each of next 2 tr, 1ss in next 2ch sp, 3ch (counts as first tr), 4tr in same sp, 1tr in centre st of next 3tr group, *5tr in next 2ch sp, 1tr in centre st of next 3tr group; rep from * twice more, join with a ss in top of first 3ch.
ROUND 3: 1ss in each of next 2 tr, 3ch, 5tr in same place as last ss (centre st of 5tr group), miss 2 tr, 3tr in next tr (centre of side edge), *6tr in centre st of next 5tr group, miss 2 tr, 3tr in next tr; rep from * twice more, join with a ss in top of first 3ch.
ROUND 4: 1ss in each of next 2 tr, 1ss in sp between 3rd and 4th tr of this 6tr corner group, 3ch, 5tr in same sp, 3tr in each sp between 3tr groups to next 6tr corner group, *6tr in sp between 3rd and 4th tr of next 6tr group, 3tr in each sp between 3tr groups to next 6tr corner group; rep from * to end, join with a ss in top of first 3ch.
Rep Round 4 until same number of rounds have been worked as on front.
Fasten off.

Finishing

Front:
ROUND 1: With RS facing and using A, join yarn in sp between 3rd and 4th tr of any 6tr corner group, 1ch, 2dc in same place, 1dc in each tr to next 6tr group, *1tr in each of first 3 tr of 6tr group, [2dc, 1ch, 2dc] in sp between 3rd and 4th tr of this 6tr group, 1dc

in each tr to next 6tr corner group; rep from * twice more, 2dc in same corner as first 2dc of round, 1ch, join with a ss in first dc of round.
Fasten off.
Back:
ROUND 1: With RS facing and using A, work as for front.
Fasten off.
Join Front and Back:
ROUND 2: With front and back WS together and working all sts through both pieces, join A with a ss in any 1ch corner sp, 1ch, [2dc, 1ch, 2dc] in same sp, 1dc in each st to next 1ch corner sp, *[2dc, 1ch, 2dc] in next 1ch sp, 1dc in each st to next 1ch corner sp; rep from * twice more (inserting cushion pad before closing last side), join with a ss in first dc.
Do not fasten off.
Crown edging:
ROUND 3: 3ch, miss 1 dc, 2trCL picot in next 1ch corner sp, 3ch, miss 2 dc, 1dc in next dc, *3ch, miss 1 dc, 2trCL picot in next dc, 3ch, miss 1 dc, 1dc in next dc*; rep from * to * to next '2ch, 1ch, 2dc' corner group, **3ch, miss 2 dc, 2trCL picot in 1ch corner sp, 3ch, miss 2 dc, 1dc in next dc**; rep from * to * along each edge and from ** to ** at each corner to end, join with a ss in base of first 3ch.
Fasten off.

ROUND 3: Join C with a ss in centre st of any 5tr group, 3ch, 5tr in same st, miss 2 tr, 3tr in next tr (centre of side edge), *6tr in centre st of next 5tr group, miss 2 tr, 3tr in next tr; rep from * twice more, join with a ss in top of first 3ch.
Fasten off C.
ROUND 4: Join D with a ss in sp between 3rd and 4th tr of any 6tr group, 3ch, 5tr in same sp, [3tr in next sp between next two 3tr groups] twice, *6tr in sp between 3rd and 4th tr of next 6tr group, 3tr in each of next 2 sps; rep from * twice more, join with a ss in top of first 3ch.
Fasten off D.
ROUND 5: Join E (main colour) with a ss in sp between 3rd and 4th tr of any 6tr group, 3ch, 5tr in same sp, [3tr in next sp] 3 times, *6tr in sp between 3rd and 4th tr of next 6tr group, [3tr in next sp] 3 times; rep from * twice more, join with a ss in top of first 3ch.
Do not fasten off, but cont with E to complete front.
ROUND 6: 1ss in each of next 2 tr, 1ss in sp between 3rd and 4th tr of this 6tr group, 3ch, 5tr in same sp, 3tr in each sp between 3tr groups to next 6tr corner group, *6tr in

Tip

For a larger mat, continue as set until the mat measures the desired size.

MATERIALS

MATS
DMC Hoooked Zpagetti (92% recycled cotton/8% other recycled fibres)
- 1 x ball – approx 120m (131yd) – each of Pink (**A**), Pink Red (**B**), Fuchsia (**C**) and White (**D**)

FLOWERS
DMC Natura Just Cotton (100% cotton)
- 1 x 50g (1¾oz) ball – approx 155m (169½yd) – each of N27 Star Light (**E**), N17 Avessac (**F**), N43 Golden Lemon (**G**) and N01 Ibiza (**H**)
Rowan Cotton Glacé (100% cotton)
- 1 x 50g (1¾oz) ball – approx 115m (125yd) – each of 724 Bubbles (**J**) and 814 Shoot (**K**)

- 3.5mm (US size E/4) and 9mm (US size M/13) crochet hooks
- Sewing needle and thread to match each petal colour

ABBREVIATIONS

ch	chain
cont	continu(e)(ing)
dc	double crochet
rep	repeat
RS	right side
ss	slip stitch
st(s)	stitch(es)
tr	treble

MEASUREMENTS

Approx 33cm (13in) in diameter

TENSION

7 sts x 7 rows over a 10cm (4in) square working dc using 9mm (US size M/13) hook.

NOTE

This is made using a fabric yarn with strands that are inconsistent in thickness. The pattern is a guide to making the mats but if your work begins to go wavy make one row of double crochet without increasing and then increase on the next round, which will keep the mat flat.

This is an Intermediate level pattern because it's quite tricky to use a thicker hook and yarn, even though the pattern itself is not difficult.

Place Mats

Here I've used a new yarn that is a recycled jersey cotton. You can also make these place mats by cutting up strips of fabric – it's a great opportunity to use up old shirts!

Mat

(MAKE 1 IN EACH OF A, B, C AND D)
Using 9mm (US size M/13) hook, make 6ch, join with a ss in first ch to form a ring.
ROUND 1 (RS): 1ch, 8dc in ring. (8 sts)

Cont in rounds with RS always facing. Mark first st of each round with a stitch marker to keep track of where round starts and ends.
ROUND 2: 2dc in each st. (16 sts)
ROUND 3: *2dc in next st, 1dc in next st; rep from * to end. (24 sts)

ROUND 4: 1dc in each st to end. (24 sts)

ROUND 5: *2dc in next st, 1dc in next st; rep from * to end. (36 sts)

ROUND 6: Rep Round 4. (36 sts)

ROUND 7: *2dc in next st, 1dc in each of next 2 sts; rep from * to end. (48 sts)

ROUND 8: Rep Round 4. (48 sts)

ROUND 9: *2dc in next st, 1dc in each of next 3 sts; rep from * to end. (60 sts)

ROUND 10: Rep Round 4. (72 sts)

ROUND 11: *2dc in next st, 1dc in each of next 4 sts; rep from * to end. (72 sts)
Fasten off.

Flower

(MAKE 16 PER MAT, USING ANY TWO OF THE SIX COLOURS – E, F, G, H, J AND K – FOR EACH MAT)

NOTE: To make mats as they appear here – for mat in A, use E for centre and J for petals; for mat in B, use G for centre and E for petals; for mat in C, use K for centre and H for petals; for mat in D, use K for centre and F for petals.

Using 3.5mm (US size E/4) hook and first colour, make 7ch, join with a ss in first ch.

ROUND 1 (CENTRE): 1ch, 14dc in ring, join with a ss in first dc.
Fasten off first colour.

ROUND 2 (PETALS): Join second colour with a ss in any dc, [3ch, 2tr in next st, 3ch, 1ss in next st] 7 times, working last ss in base of first 3ch.
Fasten off.

Finishing

Sew in ends. Using matching sewing thread, sew one flower in centre of RS of each mat and 15 evenly spaced around the outside edge.

MATERIALS

CLOTH 1
Rooster Almerino DK (50% baby alpaca/50% merino wool) DK
(light worsted) yarn
● 1 x 50g (1¾oz) ball – approx 112.5m (123yd) – each of
210 Custard (**A**), 211 Brighton Rock (**B**), 203 Strawberry Cream (**C**),
208 Ocean (**D**), 205 Glace (**E**) and 217 Beach (**F**)

CLOTH 2
Rooster Almerino DK (50% baby alpaca/50% merino wool) DK
(light worsted) yarn
● 1 x 50g (1¾oz) ball – approx 112.5m (123yd) – each of
216 Pier (**A**), 203 Strawberry Cream (**B**), 211 Brighton Rock (**C**),
219 Sandcastle (**E**) and 210 Custard (**F**)
Debbie Bliss Rialto DK (100% extra-fine merino wool) DK (light
worsted) yarn
● 1 x 50g (1¾oz) ball – approx 105m (115yd) – of 10 Moss (**D**)

● 4mm (US size G/6) crochet hook
● 30 x 40cm (12 x 16in) of lining fabric for each cloth
● 22.5cm (9in) square of heat-resistant cloth, for each cloth
● Sewing needle and thread to match lining

ABBREVIATIONS

ch	chain
cont	continu(e)(ing)
dc	double crochet
rep	repeat
RS	right side
sp(s)	space(s)
ss	slip stitch
st(s)	stitch(es)
tr	treble
WS	wrong side
yrh	yarn round hook

SPECIAL ABBREVIATIONS

2trCL (2 treble cluster) – [yrh, insert hook in st (or sp), yrh, pull
yarn through, yrh, pull yarn through first 2 loops on hook] twice in
same st, yrh, pull yarn through all 3 loops on hook.
3trCL (3 treble cluster) – [yrh, insert hook in st (or sp), yrh, pull
yarn through, yrh, pull yarn through first 2 loops on hook] 3 times
in same st, yrh, pull yarn through all 4 loops on hook.

MEASUREMENTS

Each cloth 21.5cm (8½in) square

TENSION

First 5 rounds of cloth measure 9.5cm (3¾in) square using 4mm
(US size G/6) hook.

Oven Cloths

These cloths are such a pretty addition to anyone's
kitchen. I much prefer them to oven gloves –
I usually need to get into the oven in a hurry and
don't have time to put on gloves. I can't believe
I haven't designed something like these before!

Cloth

Using A, make 4ch, join with a ss in first ch to form a ring.
ROUND I (RS): 1ch, 8dc in ring, break off A, join in B with a ss in first dc.
Cont in rounds with RS always facing.

ROUND 2: 3ch, 1tr in same place as last ss (these 3ch and 1tr count as first 2trCL), 2ch, *2trCL in next dc, 2ch; rep from * to end, join with a ss in first tr. (8 clusters)
Fasten off B.

ROUND 3: Join C with a ss in any 2ch sp, 3ch, [3trCL, 3ch, 1ss] in same sp as last ss (1 petal made), 1dc in top of next 2trCL, *[1ss, 3ch, 3trCL, 4ch, 1ss] in next 2ch sp, 1dc in top of next 2trCL; rep from * to end, join with a ss in same sp as first petal. (8 petals)
Fasten off C.

ROUND 4: Join D with a ss in any dc between petals, 1ch, 1dc in same st, *keeping petal at front of work, 3ch, 1dc in next dc (between petals), 2ch, 1dc in next dc; rep from * to end, join with a ss in first dc. (8 ch sps)
Do not fasten off, but cont with D for next round.

ROUND 5: 1ss in first 3ch sp, 3ch (counts as 1tr), [2tr, 2ch, 3tr] in same sp (corner), *1ch, 2tr in next 2ch sp, 1ch, [3tr, 2ch, 3tr] in next 3ch sp (corner); rep from * to last 2ch sp, 1ch, 2tr in last 2ch sp, 1ch, join with a ss in top of first 3ch.
Fasten off D.

ROUND 6: Join E in any 2ch corner sp, 3ch (counts as 1tr), [2tr, 2ch, 3tr] in same sp (corner), 3tr in each of next two 1ch sps, *[3tr, 2ch, 3tr] in next 2ch corner sp, 3tr in each of next two 1ch sps; rep from * to end, join with a ss in top of first 3ch.
Fasten off E.

ROUND 7: Join F in any 2ch corner sp, 3ch (counts as 1tr), [2tr, 2ch, 3tr] in same sp (corner), [3tr in sp between next two 3tr groups] 3 times, *[3tr, 2ch, 3tr] in next 2ch corner sp, [3tr in sp between next two 3tr groups] 3 times; rep from * to end, join with a ss in top of first 3ch.
Do not fasten off, but cont with F to complete cloth.

ROUND 8: 1ss in each of next 2 tr, 1ss in next 2ch sp, 3ch (counts as 1tr), [2tr, 2ch, 3tr] in same sp (corner), 3tr in each sp between 3tr groups to next '3tr, 2ch, 3tr' corner group, *[3tr, 2ch, 3tr] in next 2ch corner sp, 3tr in each sp between 3tr groups to next '3tr, 2ch, 3tr' corner group; rep from * to end, join with a ss in top of first 3ch.

ROUNDS 9–12: Rep Round 8.
Fasten off.

Finishing

Sew in ends.
Block and steam.

Tab:
Cut a piece of lining fabric 12 x 21cm (4¾ x 8 ¼in). Fold in half lengthways with WS together and press, then open out. Fold both long raw edges to meet at the centre foldline and press. Fold the tab in half again along the first foldline to conceal the long raw edges and then sew together along the open long edge.
Fold the tab in half widthways to create a loop and set aside.

Lining:
Cut a piece of lining fabric 1.5cm (5/8in) larger all around than the finished oven cloth and a piece of heat-resistant fabric the same size as the oven cloth. Fold under and press a hem of 1.5cm (5/8in) along each edge of the lining fabric. Place the heat-resistant fabric on the lining with WS together, slip the raw ends of the tab in between the heat-resistant fabric and the lining in one corner, pin and machine sew around all four sides securing the tab at the same time.
Place the heat-resistant side of the lining on the WS of the oven cloth. Pin and hand sew around all four edges.

Buggy Blanket

This is a really colourful and eye-catching blanket for a buggy or a car seat. It's not very difficult to make – once you've mastered the first square, the rest is easy.

COLOUR COMBINATIONS

Make 8 of each colourway.
SQUARE 1: Col 1 = A, Col 2 = B, Col 3 = C, Col 4 = D, Col 5 = J
SQUARE 2: Col 1 = E, Col 2 = H, Col 3 = A, Col 4 = F, Col 5 = B
SQUARE 3: Col 1 = A, Col 2 = B, Col 3 = E, Col 4 = F, Col 5 = G
SQUARE 4: Col 1 = A, Col 2 = D, Col 3 = J, Col 4 = F, Col 5 = E
SQUARE 5: Col 1 = A, Col 2 = E, Col 3 = C, Col 4 = F, Col 5 = A
SQUARE 6: Col 1 = A, Col 2 = J, Col 3 = G, Col 4 = F, Col 5 = C

Squares

(MAKE 48)

Using Col 1, 4ch, join with a ss in first ch to form a ring.
ROUND 1 (RS): 1ch, 8dc in ring, break off Col 1, join in Col 2 with a ss in first dc. Cont in rounds with RS always facing.
ROUND 2: 3ch, 1tr in same place as last ss (counts as first 2trCL), 2ch, *2trCL in next st, 2ch; rep from * to end, join with a ss in first tr. (8 clusters)
Fasten off Col 2.
ROUND 3: Join Col 3 with a ss in any 2ch sp, *3ch, [3trCL, 4ch, 1ss] in same sp (1 petal made), 1dc in top of next 2trCL, 1ss in next 2ch sp; rep from * working last ss in same sp as first petal. (8 petals)
Fasten off Col 3.
ROUND 4 (MAKE CH SPS): Join Col 4 with a ss in top of any dc between petals, 1ch, 1dc in same place as ss, *keeping petal at front of work, 3ch, 1dc in next dc (between next 2 petals), 2ch, 1dc in next dc; rep from * to end, join with a ss in first dc. (8 ch sps)

Do not fasten off, but cont with Col 4.
ROUND 5: 1ss in first 3ch sp, 3ch (counts as 1tr), [2tr, 2ch, 3tr] in same sp (corner), *1ch, 2tr in next 2ch sp, 1ch, [3tr, 2ch, 3tr] in next 3ch sp (corner); rep from * twice more, *1ch, 2tr in last 2ch sp, 1ch, join with a ss in top of first 3ch.
Fasten off Col 4.
ROUND 6: Join Col 5 with a ss in any 2ch corner sp, 3ch (counts as 1tr), [2tr, 2ch, 3tr] in same sp (corner), 3tr in each of next two 1ch sps, *[3tr, 2ch, 3tr] in 2ch corner sp, 3tr in each of next two 1ch sps; rep from * to end, join with a ss in top of first 3ch.
Fasten off.

Finishing

Sew in ends. Arrange squares in eight horizontal rows of six squares each, using all six colourways in each row but arranging them randomly. With WS together, hand sew squares together in rows of six using a backstitch and then sew eight rows together.
Edging:
Join J with a ss in any corner sp, 1ch, 3dc in same sp, *1dc in each st of first square to corner ch sp of first seam, 1dc in ch sp (at end of first square), [1dc in next ch sp (of next square), 1dc in each st to corner ch sp of same square, 1dc in ch sp] rep to next corner of blanket, 2dc in same corner sp; rep from * to end, join with a ss in first dc.
Fasten off.

MATERIALS

Rooster Almerino DK (50% baby alpaca/50% merino wool) DK (light worsted) yarn
● 2 x 50g (1¾oz) balls – approx 225m (246yd) – each of 210 Custard (**A**), 211 Brighton Rock (**B**), 203 Strawberry Cream (**C**), 208 Ocean (**D**), 220 Lighthouse (**E**), 207 Gooseberry (**F**) and 215 Lilac Sky (**G**)
● 1 x 50g (1¾oz) ball – approx 112.5m (123yd) – each of 218 Starfish (**H**), 217 Beach (**J**) and 204 Grape (**K**)
● 5mm (US size H/8) crochet hook
● Yarn sewing needle

ABBREVIATIONS

ch	chain
Col	colour
dc	double crochet
rep	repeat
RS	right side
sp(s)	space(s)
ss	slip stitch
st(s)	stitch(es)
tr	treble
WS	wrong side
yrh	yarn round hook

SPECIAL ABBREVIATIONS

2trCL (2 treble cluster) – [yrh, insert hook in st, yrh, pull yarn through, yrh, pull through first 2 loops on hook] twice in same st, yrh, pull through all 3 loops on hook.

3trCL (3 treble cluster) – [yrh, insert hook in st, yrh, pull yarn through, yrh, pull through first 2 loops on hook] 3 times in same st, yrh, pull through all 4 loops on hook.

MEASUREMENTS

48 x 64cm (19½ x 26in)

TENSION

Each square measures 8 x 8cm (3¼ x 3¼in) using 5mm (US size H/8) hook.

Chevron and Daisy Scarf

This is a really lovely stitch to use and the wave stitch is fast to work. The design makes a great scarf for men or women; for a man just omit the flowers!

Scarf

Using A and 4.5mm (US size 7) hook, make 26ch.

ROW I (RS): 1dc in 2nd ch from hook, 1dc in each ch to end. (25 sts)

ROW 2: 1ch, 1dc in first dc, *1htr in next dc, 1tr in next dc, 3dtr in next dc, 1tr in next dc, 1htr in next dc, 1dc in next dc; rep from * to end.

ROW 3: 1ch, dc2tog over first 2 sts (dc and htr), 1dc in each of next 2 sts, 3dc in next st (centre dtr of 3dtr group), 1dc in each of next 2 sts, *dc3tog over next 3 sts, 1dc in each of next 2 sts, 3dc in next st, 1dc in each of next 2 sts; rep from * to last 2 sts, dc2tog over last 2 sts (htr and dc).

ROW 4: 1ch, dc2tog over first 2 dc (dc and htr), 1dc in each of next 2 dc, 3dc in next dc (centre dc of 3dc group), 1dc in each of next 2 dc, *dc3tog over next 3 dc, 1dc in each of next 2 dc, 3dc in next dc, 1dc in each of next 2 dc; rep from * to last 2 sts, dc2tog over last 2 dc.

ROW 5: 4ch, miss first st, 1dtr in next st, 1tr in next st, 1htr in next st, 1dc in next st (centre dc of 3dc group), 1htr in next st, 1tr in next st,

MATERIALS

Rooster Almerino Aran (50% baby alpaca/50% merino wool) Aran (worsted) yarn

● 6 x 50g (1¾oz) balls – approx 564m (618yd) – of 305 Custard (**A**)

● 1 x 50g (1 ¾oz) ball – approx 94m (103yd) – of 301 Cornish (**B**)

Rooster Almerino DK (50% baby alpaca/50% merino wool) DK (light worsted) yarn

● 1 x 50g (1¾oz) ball – approx 112.5m (123yd) – each of 210 Custard (**C**) and 201 Cornish (**D**)

● 3mm (US size D/3) and 4.5mm (US size 7) crochet hooks

● Sewing needle and off-white thread

ABBREVIATIONS

ch	chain
cont	continu(e)(ing)
dc	double crochet
dtr	double treble
htr	half treble
rep	repeat
patt	pattern
RS	right side
ss	slip stitch
st(s)	stitch(es)
tr	treble
yrh	yarn round hook

SPECIAL ABBREVIATIONS

dc2tog (double crochet 2 stitches together) – [insert hook in next st, yrh, pull yarn through] twice, yrh, pull through all 3 loops on hook.

dc3tog (double crochet 3 stitches together) – [insert hook in next st, yrh, pull yarn through] 3 times, yrh, pull through all 4 loops on hook.

dtr2tog (double treble 2 stitches together) – *yrh twice, insert hook in next st, yrh, pull yarn through, [yrh, pull through first 2 loops on hook] twice; rep from * once more, yrh, pull through all 3 loops on hook.

dtr3tog (double treble 3 stitches together) – *yrh twice, insert hook in next st, yrh, pull yarn through, [yrh, pull through first 2 loops on hook] twice; rep from * twice more, yrh, pull through all 4 loops on hook.

MEASUREMENTS

Approx 228 x 18.5cm (91¼ x 7¼in)

TENSION

14 sts x 11 rows over a 10cm (4in) square working Wave and Chevron patt using 4.5mm (US size 7) hook.

*dtr3tog over next 3 sts, 1tr in next st, 1htr in next st, 1dc in next st, 1htr in next st, 1tr in next st; rep from * to last 2 sts, dtr2tog over last 2 sts.

ROW 6: 1ch, 1dc in each st to end, working last dc in last dtr. (25 sts)

ROW 7: 1ch, 1dc in each dc to end.

ROWS 8-13: Rep Rows 2–7 once.

ROWS 14-17: Rep Rows 2–5 once.
Break off A, but do not fasten off.

ROWS 18-19: Join in B and rep Rows 6 and 7.
Break off B, but do not fasten off.

ROW 20: Join in A and rep Row 2.
[Rep Rows 3–20] 12 times more, then Rows 3–19 once – work measures approx 228cm (91¼in).
Do not fasten off, but cont with A to work edging as follows.

Edging:
With RS facing and using A and 4.5mm (US size 7) hook, work 2dc in corner, then work dc evenly along row-end edge, 2dc in corner, 1dc in each foundation ch, 2dc in corner, work dc evenly along remaining row-end edge, 2 dc in corner, join with a ss in first dc of last row of scarf.
Fasten off.

Flowers

(MAKE 13)

Using C and 3mm (US size D/3) hook, make 4ch, join with a ss in first ch to form a ring.

ROUND 1 (RS): 1ch, 11dc in ring, break off C, join in D with a ss in first dc.
Cont with RS facing.

ROUND 2: 11ch, 1ss in same dc as last ss, [11ch, 1ss in next dc] 11 times, join with a ss at base of first 11ch. (12 petals)
Fasten off.

Finishing

Sew in ends. On flowers, weave around centre hole to close.
The WS and RS is not hugely different on this scarf, so sew the flowers on either side in the centre of each off-white line, using sewing thread around the tips of each petal and in centre to secure.

MATERIALS

Rooster Almerino DK (50% baby alpaca/50% merino wool) DK (light worsted) yarn
● 1 x 50g (1¾oz) ball – approx 112.5m (123yd) – each of 201 Cornish (**A**) and 203 Strawberry Cream (**B**)
● 4mm (US size G/6) crochet hook
● 68cm (27in) of 1.5cm (⅝in) wide ribbon
● 23.5 x 28.5cm (9¼ x 11¼in) floral lining
● 13.5 x 28.5cm (5¼ x 11¼in) contrast pocket lining
● Sewing needle and matching thread
● 6.5cm (2¼in) square of white felt
● Approx 44 x 4mm (size 6) white seed beads

ABBREVIATIONS

beg beginning
ch chain
cont continu(e)(ing)
dc double crochet
dtr double treble
patt(s) pattern(s)
rep repeat
RS right side
ss slip stitch
st(s) stitch(es)
tr treble
WS wrong side
yrh yarn round hook

SPECIAL ABBREVIATIONS

CL (cluster) – *yrh, insert hook in next st, yrh, pull yarn through, yrh, pull through first 2 loops on hook*, work from * to * over the number of sts given on patt rows, yrh and pull through all loops on hook.

PB (place bead) – slide one bead close to the loop on the hook and continue with pattern, this will attach the bead and secure it in position.

MEASUREMENTS

20.5 x 25.5cm (8 x 10in)

TENSION

2 patts measure 10cm (4in) and 8 rows measure 8cm (3⅛in) working Catherine Wheel st using 4mm (US size G/6) hook.

Beaded Craft Kit Roll

Made with my favourite Catherine Wheel stitch, this kit roll is soft and feminine. Don't be put off by the beading – it's very simple.

Roll

Using A, make 37ch.
ROW 1: 1dc in 2nd ch from hook, 1dc in next ch, *miss 3 ch, 7tr in next ch, miss 3 ch, 1dc in each of next 3 ch; rep from * to last 4 ch, miss 3 ch, 4tr in last ch. Break off A, but do not fasten off.
ROW 2: Join in B, 1ch, 1dc in each of first 2 sts, *3ch, 1CL over next 7 sts, 3ch, 1dc in each of next 3 sts; rep from * to last 4 sts, 3ch, 1CL over last 4 sts. Cont with B.
ROW 3: 3ch (counts as 1tr), 3tr in top of 4trCL, *miss 3 ch, 1dc in each of next 3 dc, miss 3 ch, 7tr in closing loop of next CL; rep from * to end, finishing miss 3 ch, 1dc in each of last 2 dc. Break off B, but do not fasten off.
ROW 4: Join in A, 2ch (counts as 1tr) miss first st, 1CL over next 3 sts, *3ch, 1dc in each of next 3 sts, 3ch, 1CL over next 7 sts; rep from * to end, finishing 3ch, 1dc in next st, 1dc in top of first 3ch from previous row. Cont with A.
ROW 5: 1ch, 1dc in each of first 2 dc, *miss 3 ch, 7tr in closing loop of next CL, miss 3 ch, 1dc in each of next 3 dc; rep from * to end, finishing miss 3 ch, 4tr in top of first 2ch. Break off A, but do not fasten off.
Rep Rows 2–5 until work measures approx 25.5cm (10in) ending on a Row 5. Fasten off.

Edging

Thread approx 44 beads onto yarn A.
With RS facing, join A with a ss in corner at beg of long row-end edge that starts at the scalloped edge.
ROW 1 (RS): 1ch, work 39dc evenly along first long row-end edge, 2dc in corner st, work 30dc along short straight foundation-chain edge, 2dc in corner st, work 39dc evenly along second long row-end edge (do not work along scalloped edge), turn.
ROW 2 (WS): 1ch, 1dc in first st, *2ch, PB, 1ch, 1ss into 3rd ch from hook, miss 1 st, 1dc in next st; rep from * to end.
Fasten off.
With WS facing, join A with a ss in first st of second long edge, 1ch, 1dc in same place as ss, rep from * of Row 2 to end.
Fasten off.

Lining

Block and steam crochet piece.
When working on the main crochet piece from here on, the longest side becomes the width and the shortest side is the height of the kit case.
Measure crochet piece, cut main lining to same size adding 1.5cm (⅝in) on each side for hem allowances. Fold under, pin and press a 1.5cm (⅝in) hem along each side. Cut pocket (inner) lining piece the same width as main lining, but approx 10cm (4in) shorter in height. Fold under, pin, press a 1.5cm (⅝in) hem along each side. Sew along top hem of pocket using a zigzag stitch. Sew a 6 x 6.5cm (2¼ x 2½in) piece of felt

onto the end of the pocket lining along sides and bottom, using a zigzag stitch and leaving top open to use as a pocket.

Pin inner lining to main lining, matching bottom edges and leaving a 10cm (4in) gap at the top.

Machine sew inner lining to main lining along all three sides of inner lining only (sides and bottom edges) using a straight stitch close to the edge and leaving top edge of pocket lining open.

Sewing pockets:

Make pockets by machine stitching vertical lines at intervals large enough for two crochet hooks, a pair of scissors, a tape measure and two pencils.

Pin the whole lining piece onto the crochet piece with WS of lining to WS of crocheted piece.

Finishing

Cut ribbon length in half. Insert approx 2.5cm (1in) of one end of one piece between the lining and crocheted piece, in centre of left-hand side (with lining facing).

Hand sew lining onto crochet piece, using whip stitch, securing the end of the ribbon. Starting from the opposite end to the ribbon, roll up the kit case. Pin and sew other ribbon end onto the crochet piece to correspond with first ribbon end. Insert kit items into case and tie with ribbon.

Baby Blanket

Delicate and light, this shell stitch blanket is made in a soft yarn with pretty flowers around the edging.

MATERIALS
Rooster Almerino Baby (50% baby alpaca/50% merino wool)
● 8 x 50g (1¾oz) balls – approx 1000m (1092yd) – of 508 Surf (**A**)
● 1 x 50g (1¾oz) ball – approx 125m (136½yd) – each of 501 Sea Spray (**B**) and 515 Jellyfish (**C**)
● 4mm (US size G/6) crochet hook

ABBREVIATIONS
ch	chain
cont	continu(e)(ing)
dc	double crochet
rep	repeat
sp(s)	space(s)
ss	slip stitch
st(s)	stitch(es)
tr	treble
RS	right side

MEASUREMENTS
91 x 71.5cm (35¾ x 28½in)

TENSION
Approx 3 shells (20 sts) x 10½ rows over a 10cm (4in) square working shell pattern using 4mm (US size G/6) hook.

Blanket

Using A, make 129ch.
ROW 1 (RS): 3tr in third ch from hook, miss 3 ch, 1dc in each of next 7 ch, *miss 3 ch, 7tr in next ch, miss 3 ch, 1dc in each of next 7 ch; rep from * to last 4 ch, miss 3 ch, 4tr in last ch.
ROW 2: 1ch, 1dc in each st, ending 1dc in top of first 3ch in previous row.
ROW 3: 1ch, 1dc in each of first 4 sts, *miss 3 sts, 7tr in next st, miss 3 sts, 1dc in each of next 7 sts; rep from * to last 11 sts, miss 3 sts, 7tr in next st, miss 3 sts, 1dc in each of last 4 sts.
ROW 4: 1ch, 1dc in each st to end.
ROW 5: 3ch (counts as 1tr), 3tr in first st, miss 3 sts, 1dc in each of next 7 sts, *miss 3 sts, 7tr in next st, miss 3 sts, 1dc in each of next 7 sts; rep from * to last 4 sts, miss 3 sts, 4tr in last st.
Rep Rows 2–5 until work measures approx 85.5cm (33½in), ending with a Row 4.
Fasten off.

Edging

With RS facing, join B with a ss in first dc at top of last row (top right-hand corner of blanket).
ROUND 1: *1ch (does NOT count as a dc), 3dc in same dc as ss, 1dc in each of remaining dc to last dc of row, 3dc in last dc (corner), then cont around blanket, work 152dc evenly along row-end edge, 3dc in first foundation ch at bottom of blanket (corner), 1dc in each of remaining foundation ch to last foundation ch (at base of first 3tr group of row), 3dc in last ch (corner), 152dc evenly along last row-end edge, join with a ss in top of first dc. (566 sts)
Break off yarn, but do not fasten off.
Cont in rounds with RS always facing.
ROUND 2: Join in C, 1ch, 1dc in same dc as ss, 1dc in each of remaining dc to end, join with a ss in first dc.
ROUND 3: 1ss in next dc (corner dc), 1ch, 3dc in same dc as ss, *1dc in each dc to next corner dc, 3dc in corner dc; rep from * twice, 1dc in each dc to end, join with a ss in first dc.
Fasten off.

ROUND 4 (FLOWER ROUND): With RS facing, join B with a ss in centre st of 3dc corner group at top right-hand corner of blanket and work along each edge as follows.

Top edge:
Turn, 4ch, join with a ss in first ch to form a ring, turn (so RS is now facing again), [2ch, 3tr, 1dc] 4 times in ring (4 petals), join with a dc in dc at base of flower (1 flower made from * to *), 1dc in each of next 11 sts, make flower, **1dc in each of next 9 sts, make flower; rep from ** 12 times more, 1dc in each dc to centre dc of 3dc corner group, 1dc in corner dc, make flower. (2 corners completed)

First side edge:
*1dc in each of next 11 sts, make flower; rep from ** to ** of top edge 15 times, 1dc in each dc to centre dc of 3dc corner group,

1dc in corner dc, make flower. (3 corners completed)

Bottom edge:
Work as for first side edge, but working from ** to ** 12 times instead of 15. (4 corners completed)

Second side edge:
Work as for first side edge, but omitting last flower, join with a ss in base of first flower of round.
Fasten off.

Finishing

Block and press.

Tip
This edging has flowers evenly spaced along the edge with a flower in each corner. It is not essential that these are even; if you are out by a stitch or two, just carry on. It will look fabulous either way.

Chapter 3
Confident
Crocheting

If you'd like to try crocheting with lace or mohair, this section is aimed at experienced crocheters, and there is a beautiful Floral Lace Scarf (page 108) or the Wash Cloths (page 118), as well as some gorgeous layered flowers on the Floral Bag (page 104). If you love the projects in this chapter and haven't yet mastered the techniques, look in our illustrated techniques section to find helpful instructions and tips on how you can improve.

Brooch

Brooches always make beautiful gifts for friends, as well as being an accessory for yourself. This brooch has a delicate vintage look in a pretty purple.

MATERIALS
Rooster Almerino Baby (50% baby alpaca/50% merino wool)
● Small amounts of 511 Anemone (**A**), 504 Seaweed (**B**) and 503 Sandcastle (**C**)
● 2.5mm (US size C/2) crochet hook
● 3 x 4mm (size 6) glass beads and matching sewing thread
● Sewing needle
● Small brooch pin

ABBREVIATIONS
ch	chain
cont	continu(e)(ing)
dc	double crochet
dtr	double treble
htr	half treble
rep	repeat
RS	right side
ss	slip stitch
st(s)	stitch(es)
tr	treble
trtr	triple treble

MEASUREMENTS
Across the widest part, the brooch measures 9cm (3½in)

TENSION
Flower layers measure approx 6cm (2½in) in diameter and each leaf is approx 4.5cm (1¾in) long using 2.5mm (US size C/2) hook.

Flower Back

Using A, make 4ch, join with a ss in first ch to form a ring.
ROUND I (RS): 1ch, 8dc in ring, join with a ss in first dc.
Cont with RS facing.
ROUND 2: *5ch, [1trtr, 1dtr, 1tr, 1dtr, 1trtr] in next dc, 5ch, 1ss in next dc; rep from * 3 times more, working last ss in base of first 5ch.
Fasten off.

Flower Front

Using A, make 4ch, join with a ss in first ch to form a ring.
ROUND I (RS): 1ch, 8dc in ring, join with a ss in first dc.
Cont with RS facing.

ROUND 2: *4ch, 4dtr in next dc, 4ch, 1ss in next dc; rep from * 3 times more, working last ss in base of first 4ch.
Fasten off.

Leaves

(MAKE 3)
Using B, make 8ch.
ROUND I (RS): 1dc in 2nd ch from hook, 1htr in next ch, 1tr in each of next 2 ch, 2tr in next ch, 1htr in next ch, 1dc in next ch, 2ch, turn work so bottom of foundation ch is at top and cont along bottom of sts just made, 1dc in first ch, 1htr in next ch, 2tr in next ch, 1tr in each of next 2 ch, 1htr in next ch, 1dc in last ch, join with a ss in tip of leaf.
Fasten off.

Finishing

Sew in ends.
Lay flower front on top of flower back, with RS facing upwards, and sew together at the centre using matching yarn. Using C, embroider four large bullion or French knots in the centre of the flower. Using matching yarn, sew leaves onto back of flower.
Sew three small beads on top of knots, using matching sewing thread.
Sew a brooch pin to the back, using sewing thread.

Floral Bag

This bag reminds me of an old carpet bag. It's great for carrying around to work on the go because the crochet flowers are small and easy. If you're handy at sewing it will help to line the bag, particularly the handles, as this will strengthen them and help to keep the bag in shape.

MATERIALS
Rooster Almerino DK (50% baby alpaca/50% merino wool) DK (light worsted) yarn
- 1 x 50g (1¾oz) ball – approx 112.5m (123yd) – each of 201 Cornish, 204 Grape, 214 Damson, 211 Brighton Rock, 203 Strawberry Cream, 219 Sandcastle, 216 Pier and 217 Beach
- 5mm (US size H/8) crochet hook
- 55 x 75cm (22 x 30in) piece of lining fabric
- Sewing needle and matching thread

ABBREVIATIONS
ch	chain
cont	continu(e)(ing)
dc	double crochet
rep	repeat
RS	right side
ss	slip stitch
st(s)	stitch(es)
tr	treble
WS	wrong side

SPECIAL ABBREVIATION
PC (popcorn) – work 4tr in same st, pull up the loop of fourth tr slightly and remove hook, then insert hook in top of first tr (picking up top two loops of st), reinsert hook in dropped loop of fourth tr (3 loops on hook), pull fourth tr through first tr and pull firmly.

MEASUREMENTS
32.5 x 30cm (13 x 12in)

TENSION
Each flower measures approx 5cm (2in) in diameter using 5mm (US size H/8) hook.

Flower

(MAKE 207 – 25 IN EACH OF 8 COLOURS, PLUS 7)
Make 3ch, join with a ss in first ch to form a ring.
ROUND 1 (RS): 1ch, 6dc in ring, join with a ss in first dc.
Cont with RS facing.
ROUND 2: *2ch, 1PC in same st place as last ss, 2ch, 1ss in next st; rep from * to end working last ss at base of first 2ch. (6 petals)
Fasten off.

Finishing

For the bag, sew 179 flowers together, with WS facing, to create a panel measuring about 35 x 63cm (13¾ x 24¾in), reserving 28 flowers in random colours for the handles. Begin by arranging the flowers in rows across the narrow width of the bag, fitting them together in a similar fashion to the hexagons on the Hexagon Flower Throw (see diagram on page 55) – starting with a row of nine, then a row of ten, then a row of nine followed by a row of ten and so on, so the flower positions are staggered. Space the colours out randomly as you arrange the flowers, and fit the petals of adjacent petals in between each other. The positioning does not need to be exact, but try to tightly fill the panel area. The top and bottom of the narrow upright shape should have a neat row of flowers because these two edges will form the top of the bag, but along the long side edges the petals will overlap past the perimeters – these uneven edges will be caught into the seams.

Fold the finished panel in half widthways with RS together to form the bag shape. Pin and sew side seams in a straight line. Turn bag RS out.

Sew together a row of 14 flowers for each handle. Pin and sew one handle end to the inside of the bag front, 5cm (2in) from one side seam and with the last flower sticking partly into the inside of the bag. Sew the other end in place the same distance from the other side seam on the front. Pin and sew the second handle to the back of the bag to match.

Lining

Handles:

Cut two pieces of fabric 4cm (1¾in) wide and long enough to fit the full length of the flower handles – approx 60cm (23¾in) long. Fold both raw edges to the WS along the long edges so they meet at the centre and press. Pin and hand sew the handle lining onto WS of the centre of the crochet handle, stitching along both long edges.

Bag:

Measure the bag from side to side, and then from one top edge around the bottom to the other top edge. Cut one rectangle of lining fabric to the same size adding 1.5cm (⅝in) extra all around the edge.

Fold lining in half widthways with pieces RS together and sew side seams.

Insert lining into crochet bag with WS together. Fold top edge of lining inward towards crochet fabric and pin in place along top edge of bag over the handle ends. Hand sew the lining to the bag along top edge.

Daisy Scarf

A delicate lace stitch scarf using an alpaca yarn. The daisies are entwined into the lace stitch and made by stitching the squares together to create a lovely, wearable scarf.

Squares

(MAKE 13)
Using A, make 4ch, join with a ss in first ch to form a ring.
ROUND 1 (RS): 1ch, 8dc in ring, break off A, join in B with a ss in first dc. (8 sts)
Cont in rounds with RS always facing.
ROUND 2: 3ch, tr2tog in same place as last ss (counts as 3trCL), [3ch, 3trCL in next dc] 7 times, 3ch, join with a ss in top of tr2tog. (8 clusters)
Fasten off B.

ROUND 3: Join C with a ss in top of any 3trCL, 3ch, 1tr in same place as ss (counts as tr2tog), *miss 3ch, [tr2tog, 5ch, tr2tog] in top of next 3trCL; rep from * 6 more times, tr2tog in same place as first tr of round, 5ch, join with a ss in top of first tr.
ROUND 4: 7ch, (counts as 1tr and 4ch), [1dc in next 5ch sp, 4ch, miss 1 3trCL, 1tr in next 3trCL, 4ch] 7 times, 1dc in next 5ch sp, 4ch, join with a ss in 3rd of first 7ch. (16 sps)
ROUND 5: 1ch, 1dc in same place as last ss, *4ch, miss 4 ch, [1dtr, 4ch, 1dtr] in next dc,

4ch, miss 4 ch, 1dc in next tr, 4ch, miss 4 ch, 1htr in next dc, 4ch, miss 4 ch, 1dc in next tr; rep from * 3 times more omitting dc at end of last rep, join with a ss in first dc.
ROUND 6: 1ch, 1dc in same place as last ss, 4dc in next ch sp, *[1tr, 3ch, 1tr] in next ch sp (corner), 4dc in next ch sp, 1dc in next dc, 4dc in next ch sp, 1dc in next htr, 4dc in next ch sp, 1dc in next dc, 4dc in next ch sp; rep from * twice more, [1tr, 3ch, 1tr] in next ch sp (corner), 4dc in next ch sp, 1dc in next dc, 4dc in next ch sp, 1dc in next htr, 4dc in next ch sp, join with a ss in first dc.
Fasten off.

Finishing

With WS together join squares together along one of each of the seams.
Edging:
ROUND 1 (RS): With RS facing, join C with a ss in top left corner sp, 1ch, 3dc in same sp, then (along first long side of scarf) work *1 dc in next tr, 1dc in each dc (19 dc in all) to next corner tr, 1dc in next tr, 1 dc in next sp, 1 dc in seam, 1 dc in next sp (at beg of next

MATERIALS

Rooster Almerino Baby (50% baby alpaca/50% merino wool)
- 1 x 50g (1¾oz) ball – approx 125m (136½yd) – each of 503 Sandcastle (**A**) and 502 Seashell (**B**)
- 3 x 50g (1¾oz) balls – approx 375m (409½yd) – of 501 Sea Spray (**C**)
- 3mm (US size D/3) crochet hook
- Yarn needle

ABBREVIATIONS

ch	chain
cont	continue
dc	double crochet
rep	repeat
sp(s)	space(s)
ss	slip stitch
st(s)	stitch(es)
tr	treble
RS	right side
yrh	yarn round hook

SPECIAL ABBREVIATIONS

3trCL (3 treble cluster) – [yrh, insert hook in st, pull yarn through, yrh, pull through first 2 loops on hook] 3 times in same st, yrh, pull through all 4 loops on hook.
tr2tog (treble 2 stitches together) – [yrh, insert hook in st, yrh, pull yarn through, yrh, pull through first 2 loops on hook] twice in same st, yrh, pull through all 3 loops on hook.

MEASUREMENTS

153.5 x 15.5cm (60 x 6in)

TENSION

Each square measures 11.5 x 11.5cm (4½ x 4½in) using 3mm (US size D/3) hook.

square)*; rep from * to * along remaining 12 squares but omitting '1dc in seam, 1dc in next sp' at end of last rep; (along first short side of scarf) work 2dc in same sp as last dc (so there are 3dc in corner sp), 1dc in next tr, 1dc in each dc (19 dc in all) to next corner tr, 1dc in next tr, 3dc in next sp; (along next long side of scarf) rep from * to * along all 13 squares but omitting '1dc in seam, 1dc in next sp' at end of last rep; (along next short side of scarf) work 2dc in same sp as last dc (so there are 3dc in corner sp), 1dc in next tr, 1dc in each dc (19 dc in all) to next corner tr, 1dc in next tr, join with a ss in first dc.
Fasten off.
Cont with RS facing.
ROUND 2: Join C with a ss to centre dc of any 3dc corner group, 8ch, (counts as first tr and 5ch), 1tr in 5th ch from hook, miss 2 sts, *1tr in next st, 5ch, 1tr in 5th ch from hook, miss 2 sts; rep from * to next corner, 1tr in centre corner st, 5ch, 1tr in 5th ch from hook, 1tr in same corner st, 5ch, 1tr in 5th ch from hook, miss 2 sts; rep from * to last corner, 1tr in centre corner st (at base of first 3ch), 5ch, 1tr in 5th ch from hook, join with a ss in 3rd of first 8ch.
Fasten off.
Sew in ends.

Floral Lace Scarf

This is a very easy stitch to achieve, but the scarf is in the higher level because of the very fine mohair yarn used – if you make a mistake, it is very difficult to undo. Practise the stitch using some scraps of double knitting or aran-weight yarn to master the techniques before you start.

Scarf

Using A and 3.5mm (US size E/4) hook, make 178ch.
ROW 1: 1dc in 6th ch from hook *5ch, miss 3 ch, 1dc in next ch; rep from * to end. (44 sps)
ROW 2: *5ch, 1dc in next 5ch sp; rep from * to end.
Rep Row 2 until work measures approx 145cm (57in) – smooth out the scarf in both directions to measure length.
Do not fasten off, but work edging as follows.
Edging:
ROUND 1 (RS): Working along first long row-end edge, work 1ch, 1dc in top of next ch (first corner), 3dc in each sp to next corner; working along short foundation-chain edge, 1dc in top of corner ch (second corner), 3dc in each sp to next corner; working along second long row-end edge, work 1dc in top of corner ch (third corner), 3dc in each sp to next corner; working along short top edge (along last row of scarf), work 1dc in top of corner ch (fourth corner), 3dc in each sp to end, join with a ss in first dc. Fasten off.
ROUND 2 (LOOP ROUND): With RS facing, join A with a ss in corner st at beg of one short edge (foundation-chain edge or 'last-row' edge), then working along first short edge, work 1ch, 1dc in same st, [16ch, 1dc in next st, 1dc in each of next 6 sts, 4ch, 1dc in same place as last dc,

*1dc in each of next 5 sts, 16ch, 1dc in same place as last dc, 1dc in each of next 5 sts, 4ch, 1dc in same place as last dc, rep from * to corner, 1dc in each dc to corner, 1dc in corner, 16ch, 1dc in next st – 27 loops made]; working along first long edge, ***measure this edge and place pin markers equally spaced apart in 31 places (for loops), then work 1dc in each st to pin marker, **at pin marker work 4ch, 1dc in same place as last dc, 1dc in each st to next pin marker, rep from ** to next corner***; working along second short edge, work 1dc in corner, rep between square brackets; working along second long edge, rep from *** to ***, join with a ss in first dc. Fasten off.

Large Flowers

(MAKE 29 TWO-COLOUR FLOWERS AND 25 ONE-COLOUR FLOWERS)
Using B or C and 3mm (US size D/3) hook, make 6ch, join with a ss in first ch to form a ring.
ROUND 1 (RS): 15dc in ring, enclosing yarn tail inside all dc around circle, break off yarn, join in B or C with a ss in first dc. Cont with RS facing.
ROUND 2: *3ch, 1tr in each of next 2 sts, 3ch, 1ss in next st; rep from * 4 times more, working last ss in first dc. (5 petals)
Fasten off.
Pull tail to close up centre hole or sew hole to close with a yarn needle.

Small Flowers

(MAKE 62)

Using B and 3mm (US size D/3) hook, make 4ch, join with a ss in first ch to form a ring.

ROUND I: [3ch, 1ss in ring] 5 times, join with a ss in base of first 3ch.

Fasten off.

Sew around hole in centre to close.

Finishing

Sew in ends.

Sew a large flower onto tip of each loop made on Round 2 of edging along short ends of scarf.

Using C, embroider one French knot in centre of each small flower. Sew small flowers onto loops made on Round 2 of edging along long edges of scarf.

When all flowers are stitched on, sew adjacent petals of large flowers to each other.

Vintage-style Vase Coaster

Vintage crochet mats are very popular at the moment, so why not make your own? Traditionally mats were made using very fine cotton yarn, but I've used double-knitting-weight cotton for a much quicker project. The pattern is a little intricate, but the stitches are easy. Make sure you block and press when finished.

Mat

Using A, make 6ch, join with a ss in first ch to form a ring.

ROUND 1 (RS): 3ch (counts as 1tr), 2tr in ring, 2ch, [3tr, 2ch] 5 times in ring, join with a ss in top of first 3ch.
Fasten off A.
Cont in rounds with RS always facing.

ROUND 2: Join B with a ss in any 2ch sp, 3ch, [2tr, 2ch, 3tr] in same 2ch sp, 1ch, *[3tr, 2ch, 3tr, 1ch] in next 2ch sp; rep from * 4 times, join with a ss in top of first 3ch.
Fasten off B.

ROUND 3: Join C with a ss in any 1ch sp, 3ch (counts as 1tr), 2tr in same 1ch sp, 1ch, *[3tr, 2ch, 3tr, 1ch] in next 2ch sp, 3tr in next 1ch sp, 1ch; rep from * 4 times, [3tr, 2ch, 3tr, 1ch] in next 2ch sp, join with a ss in top of first 3ch. Break off C, but do not fasten off.

ROUND 4: Join in D, 1ss in next tr (centre st of 3tr group), 3ch (counts as 1tr), 2tr in same place as ss just worked, 1dc in next 1ch sp, 1ch, *[1tr, 1ch] 6 times in next 2ch sp, 1dc in next 1ch sp**, 3tr in centre st of next 3tr group, 1dc in next 1ch sp, 1ch; rep from * ending last rep at **, join with a ss in top of first 3ch. Break off D, but do not fasten off.

ROUND 5: Join in E, 4ch (counts as 1dtr), 1tr in top of first 3ch in previous round, 1tr in each of next 2 tr, 1dtr in next dc, *4ch, 1dc in 1ch sp in centre of next 6tr group, 4ch**, 1dtr in next dc, 1tr in each of next 3 tr, 1dtr in next dc; rep from * ending last rep at **, join with a ss in top of first 4ch.
Do not fasten off.

ROUND 6: Cont with E, 3ch (counts as 1tr), *1tr in each of next 3 tr, 1tr in next dtr, 7tr in next 4ch sp, miss next dc, 7tr in next 4ch sp**, 1tr in next dtr; rep from * ending last rep at **, join with a ss in top of first 3ch. Break off E, but do not fasten off.

ROUND 7: Join in B (or D), 1ch, *miss next 2 tr, [2tr, 2ch, 2tr] in next tr, miss next 2 tr, 1dc in next tr; rep from * omitting dc at end of last rep, join with a ss in top of first tr at beg of round.
Do not fasten off.

ROUND 8: Cont with B (or D), 3ch (counts as 1tr), 1tr in next tr, *[2tr, 2ch, 2tr] in next 2ch sp, 1tr in each of next 2 tr**, miss next dc, 1tr in each of next 2 tr; rep from * ending last rep at **, join with a ss in top of first 3ch.
Fasten off B (or D).

ROUND 9 (FLOWER ROUND): Join A with a ss in any 2ch sp, 1ch, 1dc in same 2ch sp, *4ch, form a ring by joining with a ss in first ch of 4ch just made, [3ch, 1tr in ring, 3ch, 1ss in ring] 5 times (5 petals – 1 flower – made), 1ss in dc at base of flower, 1dc in each of next 8 tr**, 1dc in next 2ch sp; rep from * ending last rep at **, join with a ss in first dc.
Fasten off.

Finishing

Block, starch and press.

MATERIALS

MAT 1

Rowan Cotton Glacé (100% cotton)

● 1 x 50g (1¾oz) ball – approx 115m (125yd) – each of 832 Persimmon (**A**), 725 Ecru (**B**), 841 Garnet (**C**), 845 Shell (**D**) and 814 Shoot (**E**)

MAT 2

Rowan Cotton Glacé (100% cotton)

● 1 x 50g (1¾oz) ball – approx 115m (125yd) – each of 724 Bubbles (**A**), 845 Shell (**B**), 841 Garnet (**C**), 725 Ecru (**D**) and 833 Ochre (**E**)

● 3mm (US size D/3) crochet hook

ABBREVIATIONS

ch	chain
cont	continu(e)ing
dc	double crochet
dtr	double treble
rep	repeat
RS	right side
sp(s)	space(s)
ss	slip stitch
st(s)	stitch(es)
tr	treble

MEASUREMENTS

28cm (11in) in diameter

TENSION

First 4 rounds of mat pattern measure 13.5cm (5¼in) in diameter using 3mm (US size D/3) hook.

Tip

When working on the flower round, make sure that you are always working with the right side facing you.

Round Rose Cushio

The roses to cover both sides of this cushion cover use a lot of yarn, but it's a great opportunity to use up any scraps because each rose requires very little yarn – you can make around ten roses per ball of double knit wool.

MATERIALS

CUSHION COVER
Debbie Bliss Cashmerino Aran (55% merino wool, 33% microfibre, 12% cashmere) Aran (worsted) yarn
● 3 x 50g (1¾oz) balls – approx 270m (295½yd) – of 27 Stone (**MC**)

ROSES
Rooster Almerino Aran (50% baby alpaca/50% merino wool) Aran (worsted) yarn
● 2 x 50g (1¾oz) balls – approx 188m (206yd) – each of 305 Custard (17 roses), 319 Lilac Sky (14 roses) and 307 Brighton Rock (11 roses)
● 3 x 50g (1¾oz) balls – approx 282m (309yd) – each of 318 Coral (22 roses), 313 Cherry (21 roses), 301 Cornish (28 roses) and 306 Gooseberry (25 roses)
Debbie Bliss Rialto Aran (100% extra fine merino wool) Aran (worsted) yarn
● 1 x 50g (1¾oz) ball – approx 80m (87½yd) – of 35 Blossom (10 roses)
Debbie Bliss Rialto DK (100% extra fine merino wool) DK (light worsted) yarn
● 1 x 50g (1¾oz) ball – approx 105m (115yd) – of 50 Deep Rose (10 roses)
● 2 x 50g (1¾oz) balls – approx 210m (230yd) – of 42 Pink (11 roses)

● 4mm (US size G/6) and 5mm (US size H/8) crochet hooks
● Large glass-headed pin
● Yarn sewing needle
● 40cm (16in) round cushion pad

ABBREVIATIONS

ch	chain	**RS**	right side
cont	continu(e)(ing)	**ss**	slip stitch
dc	double crochet	**st(s)**	stitch(es)
dtr	double treble	**tr**	treble
rep	repeat	**WS**	wrong side

MEASUREMENTS

To fit a cushion pad approx 40cm (16in) in diameter

TENSION

14 tr x 8 rows over a 10cm (4in) square working tr using 5mm (US size H/8) hook.

Cover

(MAKE 2 THE SAME)
Using MC and 5mm (US size H/8) hook, make 6ch, join with a ss in first ch to form a ring.
ROUND 1 (RS): 3ch (counts as first tr), 11tr in circle, join with a ss in top of first 3ch. (12 sts)
Cont in rounds with RS always facing.
ROUND 2: 3ch, 1tr in base of first 3ch, 2tr in next and every st to end of round, join with a ss in top of first 3ch. (24 sts)
ROUND 3: 3ch, 1tr in base of first 3ch, *1tr in next st, 2tr in each of next 2 sts; rep from * to last 2 sts, 1tr in next st, 2tr in last st, join with a ss in top of first 3ch. (40 sts)
ROUND 4: 3ch, 1tr in base of first 3ch, *1tr in each of next 3 sts, 2tr in next st; rep from * to last 3 sts, 1tr in each of last 3 sts, join with a ss in top of first 3ch. (50 sts)
ROUND 5: 3ch, 1tr in base of first 3ch, *1tr in each of next 4 sts, 2tr in next st; rep from * to last 4 sts, 1tr in each of last 4 sts, join with a ss in top of first 3ch. (60 sts)
ROUND 6: 3ch, 1tr in base of first 3ch *1tr in each of next 5 sts, 2tr in next st; rep from * to last 5 sts, 1tr in each of last 5 sts, join with a ss in top of first 3ch. (70 sts)
ROUND 7: 3ch, 1tr in base of first 3ch, *1tr in each of next 6 sts, 2tr in next st; rep from * to last 6 sts, 1tr in each of last 6 sts, join with a ss in top of first 3ch. (80 sts)
ROUND 8: 3ch, 1tr in base of first 3ch, *1tr in each of next 7 sts, 2tr in next st; rep from * to last 7 sts, 1tr in each of last 7 sts, join with a ss in top of first 3ch. (90 sts)
ROUND 9: 3ch, 1tr in base of first 3ch, *1tr in each of next 8 sts, 2tr in next st; rep from * to last 8 sts, 1tr in each of last 8 sts, join with a ss in top of first 3ch. (100 sts)
ROUND 10: Rep Round 5. (120 sts)
ROUND 11: 3ch, 1tr in base of first 3ch *1tr in each of next 11 tr, 2tr in next st; rep from * to last 11 tr, 1tr in each of last 11 tr, join with a ss in top of first 3ch. (130 sts)
ROUND 12: 3ch, 1tr in base of first 3ch, *1tr in each of next 12 tr, 2tr in next st; rep from * to last 12 tr, 1tr in each of last 12 tr, join with a ss in top of first 3ch. (140 sts)
ROUND 13: As Round 7. (160 sts)
ROUND 14: 3ch, 1tr in base of first 3ch, *1tr in each of next 15 tr, 2tr in next st, rep from * to last 15 tr, 1tr in each of last 15 tr, join with a ss in top of first 3ch. (170 sts)
Fasten off.

Roses

(MAKE 169 IN VARIOUS COLOURS)
Using 4mm (US size G/6) hook, make 53ch. Work all petals along 53ch with RS facing.
PETAL 1: 1tr in third ch from hook, 1tr in each of next 2 ch, 3ch, 1ss in next ch.

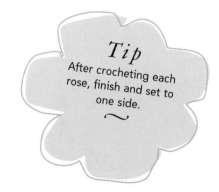

Tip
After crocheting each rose, finish and set to one side.

PETAL 2: 4ch, 1dtr in each of next 3 ch, 3ch, 1ss in next ch.
PETAL 3: 4ch, 1dtr in each of next 4 ch, 3ch, 1ss in next ch.
PETAL 4: 4ch, 1dtr in each of next 5 ch, 3ch, 1ss in next ch.
PETAL 5: 4ch, 1dtr in each of next 6 ch, 3ch, 1ss in next ch.
PETAL 6: 3ch, 1tr in each of next 2 ch, 3ch, 1ss in next ch.
PETAL 7: 4ch, 1dtr in each of next 3 ch, 3ch, 1ss in next ch.
PETAL 8: 4ch, 1dtr in each of next 4 ch, 3ch, 1ss in next ch.
PETAL 9: 4ch, 1dtr in each of next 5 ch, 3ch, 1ss in next ch.
PETAL 10: 4ch, 1dtr in each of next 6 ch, 3ch, 1ss in last ch.
Fasten off.

Finishing

To make up roses, with WS facing and starting with first petal (smallest), coil petals keeping base flat at chain edge. Insert a large glass-headed pin across base of rose to hold it in position and stitch the petals in place across the base using a yarn sewing needle and matching yarn.

Sew majority of roses onto RS of the two cover pieces, leaving enough roses to be sewn on around the seam later.

Place cover pieces WS together. Using 5mm (US size H/8) hook and MC, join yarn with a ss by inserting hook through one st in last round of both cover pieces, make 1ch, 1dc in same place as ss, then working all sts through both layers, 1dc in each st until seam is half finished, insert cushion pad and then continue in dc until seam is completed, join with a ss in first dc.

Fasten off.

Sew remaining roses around seam area.

Tip
The size of the cushion can be adjusted by working fewer or more rounds, making further increases following the same sequence in the pattern. Keep an eye on the measurement of your cushion pad as you work and stop when you achieve the size required. One 50g (1¾oz) ball will make 10 roses.

MATERIALS

Rooster Almerino DK (50% baby alpaca/50% merino wool) DK (light worsted) yarn

SQUARES

- 5 x 50g (1¾oz) balls – approx 562.5m (615yd) – of 219 Sandcastle (**A**)
- 4 x 50g (1¾oz) balls – approx 450m (492yd) – each of 211 Brighton Rock (**B**), 220 Lighthouse (**C**), 216 Pier (**D**) and 204 Grape (**E**)
- 3 x 50g (1¾oz) balls – approx 337.5m (369yd) – each of 207 Gooseberry (**F**) and 205 Glace (**G**)
- 2 x 50g (1¾oz) balls – approx 225m (246yd) – each of 215 Lilac Sky (**H**) and 203 Strawberry Cream (**J**)
- 11 x 50g (1¾oz) balls – approx 1237.5m (1353yd) – of 201 Cornish (**K**)

EDGING

- 5 x 50g (1¾oz) balls – approx 562.5m (620yd) – of 211 Brighton Rock (**B**)

- 4.5mm (US size 7) crochet hook

ABBREVIATIONS

ch	chain
Col	colour
dc	double crochet
rep	repeat
RS	right side
sp(s)	space(s)
ss	slip stitch
st(s)	stitch(es)
tr	treble
WS	wrong side
yrh	yarn round hook

SPECIAL ABBREVIATION

Loop St – with yarn over left index finger, insert hook in next st, draw 2 strands through st (take first strand from under index finger and at same time take second strand from over index finger) pull yarn to tighten loop forming a 2.5cm (1in) loop on index finger. Remove finger from loop, put loop to back (RS) of work, yrh and pull through 3 loops on hook (1 Loop St made on RS of work)

MEASUREMENTS

136 x 112cm (58½ x 45½in), excluding loop edging

TENSION

Each square measures approx 8 x 8cm (3¼ x 3¼in) using 4.5mm (US size 7) hook.

Gypsy Queen Throw

This is a glorious throw – it looks like an old English summer garden. But don't just make it for summer, as it will cheer any home in the dark winter months, too.

COLOUR COMBINATIONS

Make 25 of each colourway plus 2.

SQUARE 1: Col 1 = C, Col 2 = B, Col 3 = K, Col 4 = F

SQUARE 2: Col 1 = A, Col 2 = D, Col 3 = K, Col 4 = E

SQUARE 3: Col 1 = B, Col 2 = G, Col 3 = K, Col 4 = D

SQUARE 4: Col 1 = C, Col 2 = D, Col 3 = K, Col 4 = B

SQUARE 5: Col 1 = A, Col 2 = H, Col 3 = K, Col 4 = D

SQUARE 6: Col 1 = B, Col 2 = E, Col 3 = K, Col 4 = G

SQUARE 7: Col 1 = E, Col 2 = F, Col 3 = K, Col 4 = A

SQUARE 8: Col 1 = J, Col 2 = F, Col 3 = K, Col 4 = G

SQUARE 9: Col 1 = J, Col 2 = G, Col 3 = K, Col 4 = A

SQUARE 10: Col 1 = C, Col 2 = J, Col 3 = K, Col 4 = E

Squares

(MAKE 252)

Using Col 1, make 4ch, join with a ss in first ch to form a ring.

ROUND 1 (RS): *2ch, 4tr in ring, 1ss in ring; rep from * 3 times more. (4 petals)

Cont in rounds with RS always facing.

ROUND 2: Bend next petal forwards to work into back of petals, 1ss in back loop at base of 2nd tr of first petal of Round 1, *keeping chain loops behind petals, 4ch, 1ss in back loop at base of

2nd tr of next petal; rep from * twice more, 4ch, join with a ss in base of first 4ch. (4 loops)

ROUND 3: *[1ss, 5tr, 1ss] in next 4ch loop; rep from * 3 times more, join with a ss in first ss. (4 petals)
Fasten off Col 1.

ROUND 4: Join Col 2 with a ss in ss between any two petals, *keeping chain loops behind petals made in Round 3, 6ch, 1ss in ss between next two petals; rep from * 3 times more, working last ss in base of first 6ch.

ROUND 5: 1ss in first 6ch sp, 3ch (counts as 1tr), [2tr, 2ch, 3tr] in same sp, *1ch, [3tr, 2ch, 3tr] in next 6ch sp; rep from * twice more, 1ch, join with a ss in top of first 3ch.
Fasten off Col 2.

ROUND 6: Join Col 3 with a ss in any 2ch sp (corner), 3ch (counts as 1tr), [2tr, 2ch, 3tr] in same sp, *1ch, 3tr in next 1ch sp, 1ch, [3tr, 2ch, 3tr] in next 2ch sp (corner); rep from * twice more, 1ch, 3tr in next 1ch sp, join with a ss to top of first 3ch.
Break off Col 3, but do not fasten off.

ROUND 7: Join in Col 4, 1 ch, 1dc in same place as last ss, 1dc in each of next 2 tr, 3dc in next 2ch sp, *[1dc in each of next 3 tr, 1dc in next 1ch sp] twice, 1dc in each of next 3 tr, 3dc in next 2ch sp; rep from * twice more, [1dc in each of next 3 tr, 1dc in next 1ch sp] twice, join with a ss in first dc.
Fasten off.

Finishing

Lay out the squares with 14 squares across (width) by 18 squares down (length) in a random order. Using B and with WS together, join squares first in horizontal rows and then in vertical rows using a dc seam (see page 23).

Edgings

Double crochet edging:
Work one row of dc edging all around blanket, working 1dc in each dc and 3dc in each corner dc.
Fasten off.
Sew in ends.

Loop edging:
Work with WS facing for both Loop edging rounds.

ROUND 1 (WS): Join B with a ss in first st after corner along top, 1ch, 1 Loop St in each st, join with a ss in first st.
Fasten off.

ROUND 2 (WS): Return to the start of Round 1, join B with a ss in first st, rep Round 1.
Fasten off.

Wash Cloths

These cloths are just for the pure joy of crochet and anyone with a true passion for crocheting will love making them. What better way to wash your face or the dishes than with a flower or blossoms! When choosing the yarn a cotton is best in any thickness, but avoid using mercerised cotton because this is less absorbent.

Blossom Burst Cloth

Using A, make 5ch, join with a ss in first ch to form a ring.

ROUND 1 (RS): 4ch (counts as 1tr and 1ch), [1tr in ring, 1ch] 7 times, join with a ss in 3rd of first 4ch.

Cont in rounds with RS always facing.

ROUND 2: 3ch (counts as 1tr), 2tr in same place as last ss, [miss 1 ch, 1ch, 3tr in next tr] 7 times, 1ch, join with a ss in top of first 3ch. (8 tr-groups)

ROUND 3: 1ss in each of first 2 tr, 1ss in next ch sp, 4ch (counts as 1tr and 1ch) , [1tr, 1ch, 1tr, 1ch, 1tr] in same sp, *[1tr, 1ch] 3 times in next ch sp, 1tr in same sp; rep from * 6 times more, join with a ss in 3rd of first 4ch. (8 shell groups)

Fasten off A.

ROUND 4: Join B with a ss in 3rd 1ch sp of any shell group, 2ch, tr2tog over next sp between 2 shells and next 1ch sp (between first two trebles), *3ch, 1ss in next 1ch sp, 3ch, tr3tog over next 1ch sp of same shell, next sp between 2 shells and first 1ch sp of next shell; rep from * 6 times more, 3ch, ss in next ch sp, 3ch, join with a ss in top of first tr2tog.

ROUND 5: 5ch (counts as 1tr and 2ch), [1tr, 2ch] 3 times (working in top of same tr2tog), 1tr in same place, *[1tr, 2ch] 4 times in top of next tr3tog, 1tr in same place; rep from * 6 times more, join with a ss in 3rd of first 5ch. (8 tr-groups)

Fasten off B.

ROUND 6: Join C in 4th 2ch sp of any tr-group, 3ch, 1dtr-1trtog over next sp between tr groups and next 2ch sp (between first 2 tr of next tr group), *5ch, 1dc in next 2ch sp, 1ch, 1dc in next 2ch sp, 2ch, tr3tog over next 2ch sp, next sp between tr groups and next 2ch sp (between first 2 tr of next tr group), 2ch, 1dc in next 2ch sp, 1ch, 1dc in next 2ch sp, 5ch**, 1tr-1dtr-1trtog over next 2ch, next sp between tr group and next 2ch sp (between first 2 tr of next tr group); rep from * 3 times more, but ending last rep at **, join with a ss in first dtr.

ROUND 7: 3ch, [2tr, 2ch, 3tr] in same place as last ss (top of dtr/tr corner group), *3tr in next 5ch sp, 1tr in next 1ch sp, 3tr in each of next two 2ch sps, 1tr in next 1ch sp, 3tr in next 5ch sp, [3tr, 2ch, 3tr] in top of next tr/dtr/tr group (corner); rep from * twice more, 3tr in next 5ch sp, 1tr in next 1ch sp, 3tr in each of next two 2ch sps, 1tr in next 1ch sp, 3tr in next 5ch sp, join with a ss in top of first 3ch.

ROUND 8: 1ss in each of next 2 tr, 1ss in next 2ch corner sp, 3ch, [2tr, 2ch, 3tr] in same sp, *3tr in next sp between tr groups, [2tr in next sp between tr groups] twice, 3tr in next sp between tr groups, [2tr in next sp between tr groups] twice, 3tr in next sp between tr groups**, [3tr, 2ch, 3tr] in next 2ch corner sp; rep from * 3 times more, but ending last rep at **, join with a ss in top of first 3ch.

ROUND 9: 1ss in each of next 2 tr, 1ss in next 2ch corner sp, 3ch, [2tr, 2ch, 3tr] in same ch sp, *[3tr in next sp between tr

BLOSSOM BURST CLOTH

MATERIALS
Debbie Bliss Cotton DK (100% cotton) DK/Aran (worsted) yarn
- 1 x 50g (1¾oz) ball – approx 84m (92yd) – each of 58 Fuchsia (**A**), 02 Cream (**B**) and 68 Cloud (**C**)
- 3.5mm (US size E/4) crochet hook
- Yarn sewing needle

ABBREVIATIONS
ch	chain
cont	continu(e)(ing)
dc	double crochet
dtr	double treble
rep	repeat
RS	right side
sp(s)	space(s)
ss	slip stitch
st(s)	stitch(es)
tog	together
tr	treble
yrh	yarn round hook

SPECIAL ABBREVIATIONS
tr3tog (treble 3 stitches together) – [yrh, insert hook in sp, yrh, pull yarn through, yrh, pull through first 2 loops on hook] 3 times in same sp, yrh, pull through all 4 loops on hook.

1dtr-1trtog (double treble and treble together) – yrh twice, insert hook in sp, yrh, pull yarn through, [yrh, pull through first 2 loops on hook] twice, yrh, insert hook in next sp, yrh, pull yarn through, yrh, pull through first 2 loops on hook, yrh, pull through all 3 loops on hook.

1tr-1dtr-1trtog (treble, double treble and treble together) – yrh, insert hook in sp, yrh, pull yarn through, yrh, pull through first 2 loops on hook, yrh twice, insert hook in next sp, yrh, pull yarn through, [yrh, pull yarn through first 2 loops on hook] twice, yrh, insert hook in sp, yrh, pull yarn through, yrh, pull through first 2 loops on hook, yrh, pull through all 4 loops on hook.

MEASUREMENTS
22cm (8¾in) square

TENSION
Flower centre (Rounds 1–3) measures 9cm (3½in) in diameter using 3.5mm (US size E/4) hook and A.

From left to right:
Petal-Edged Circle
Cloth, Flower
Square Cloth, and
Blossom Burst Cloth

MATERIALS

Debbie Bliss Cotton DK (100% cotton) DK/Aran (worsted) yarn
- 1 x 50g (1¾oz) ball – approx 84m (92yd) – each of 62 Periwinkle (**A**), 58 Fuchsia (**B**), 02 Cream (**C**) and 61 Aqua (**D**)
- 3.5mm (US size E/4) crochet hook
- Yarn sewing needle

ABBREVIATIONS

ch	chain
cont	continu(e)(ing)
dc	double crochet
dtr	double treble
rep	repeat
RS	right side
sp(s)	space(s)
ss	slip stitch
st(s)	stitch(es)
tog	together
tr	treble

MEASUREMENTS

22cm (8¾in) square

TENSION

Flower at centre (Rounds 1 and 2) measures 9cm (3½in) in diameter using 3.5mm (US size E/4) hook and A.

groups] twice, 2tr in next sp between tr groups, [3tr in next sp between tr groups] twice, 2tr in next sp between tr groups, [3tr in next sp between tr groups] twice**, [3tr, 2ch, 3ch] in next 2ch corner sp; rep from * 3 times more, but ending last rep at **, join with a ss in top of first 3ch.

ROUND 10: 1ss in each of next 2 tr, 1ss in next 2ch corner sp, 3ch, [2tr, 2ch, 3tr] in same ch sp, [3tr in next sp between tr groups] twice, [2tr in next sp between tr groups] twice, 3tr in next sp between tr groups, [2tr in next sp between tr groups] twice, [3tr in next sp between tr groups] twice**, [3tr, 2ch, 3tr] in next 2ch corner sp; rep from * 3 times more, but ending last rep at **, join with a ss in top of first 3ch.
Fasten off.

Finishing

Sew in ends.
Pin and block cloth to shape.

Flower Square Cloth

Using A, make 10ch, join with a ss in first ch to form a ring.

ROUND I (RS): 7ch (counts as first dtr and first 3ch sp), [1dtr, 3ch] 11 times in ring, join with a ss in 4th of 7ch. (12 ch sps)
Cont in rounds with RS always facing.

ROUND 2: 4ch (counts as 1dtr), 3dtr in first 3ch sp (formed by last 3ch of 7ch at beg of Round 1), *4dtr around stem of next dtr (working down stem towards centre), keeping next 3ch at back of work and not working into it (this 3ch sp is missed and sits at back of flower petals), work 1dtr in centre ring, 4dtr around stem of next dtr (working up stem away from centre), 4tr in next 3ch sp; rep from * 4 times more, 4dtr around stem of next dtr (working down stem towards centre), 1dtr in centre ring, 4dtr around first 4ch (working up this ch away from centre), join with a ss in top of first 4ch. (6 petals and 6 missed ch sps behind petals)
Fasten off A.

ROUND 3: Join B with a ss in any 3ch sp behind petals, 1ch, 3dc in same sp, [3ch, 3dc in next 3ch sp behind petals] 5 times, 3ch, join with a ss in first dc.

ROUND 4: 1ch, 1dc in same place as last ss, 2dc in next dc (centre dc of 3dc group), 1dc in next dc, *4dc in next 3ch sp, 1dc in next dc, 2dc in next dc (centre dc of 3dc group), 1dc in next dc; rep from * 4 times more, 4dc in next 3ch sp, join with a ss in first dc. (48 dc)

ROUND 5: 1ch, 1dc in same place as last ss, [miss 2 dc, 1dc in next dc, 3ch] 15 times, 3ch, join with a ss in first dc. (16 sps)

ROUND 6: 1ss in next ch, 1ch, 1dc in same 3ch sp, 4ch, [1dc in next 3ch sp, 4ch] 15 times, join with a ss in first dc. (16 sps)

ROUND 7: 1ss in each of first 2 ch, 1ch, 1dc in same 4ch sp, 5ch, [1dc in next 4ch sp, 5ch] 15 times, join with a ss in first dc. (16 sps)
Fasten off B.

ROUND 8: Join C with a ss in any 5ch sp, 4ch, [2dtr, 2ch, 3dtr] in same ch sp (corner), *2ch, 1dc in next 5ch sp, [5ch, 1dc in next 5ch sp] twice, 2ch**, [3dtr, 2ch, 3dtr] in next 5ch sp (corner); rep from * twice more, then once again from * to **, join with a ss in top of first 4ch.

ROUND 9: 4ch, 1dtr in each of next 2 dtr, *[3dtr, 2ch, 3dtr] in next 2ch sp (corner), 1dtr in each of next 3 dtr, 2dtr in 2ch sp, 2ch, 1dc in next 5ch sp, 5ch, 1dc in next 5ch sp, 2ch, 2dtr in 2ch sp**, 1dtr in each of next 3 dtr; rep from * twice more, then once again from * to **, join with a ss in top of first 4ch. Fasten off C.

ROUND 10: Join D with a ss in any corner sp, 3ch, [2tr, 2ch, 3tr] in same sp (first corner), *1tr in each of next 8 dtr, 2tr in next 2ch sp, 3tr in next 5ch sp, 2tr in next 2ch sp, 1tr in each of next 8 dtr**, [3tr, 2ch, 3tr] in next corner sp; rep from * twice more, then once again from * to **, join with a ss in top of first 3ch.

ROUND 11: Ss in each of next 2 tr, 1ss in next corner sp, 3ch, [2tr, 2ch, 3tr] in same sp (first corner), *1tr in each tr to next corner sp, [3tr, 2ch, 3tr] in corner sp; rep from * twice more, 1tr in each tr to last corner, join with a ss in top of first 3ch. Fasten off.

Finishing

Sew in ends.
Using C, embroider stamens in centre of flower.
Pin and block cloth to shape.

PETAL-EDGED CIRCLE

MATERIALS

Debbie Bliss Cotton DK (100% cotton) DK/Aran (worsted) yarn
- 1 x 50g (1¾oz) ball – approx 84m (92yd) – each of 39 Teal Blue (**A**), 64 Coral (**B**) and 65 Peach (**C**)
- 3.5mm (US size E/4) crochet hook
- Yarn sewing needle

ABBREVIATIONS

ch	chain	ss	slip stitch
cont	continu(e)(ing)	st(s)	stitch(es)
dc	double crochet	tog	together
dtr	double treble	tr	treble
htr	half treble	yrh	yarn round
rep	repeat		hook
RS	right side		
sp(s)	space(s)		

SPECIAL ABBREVIATIONS

PS (puff stitch or half treble 4 stitches together in same place) – [yrh, insert hook in st, yrh, pull yarn through] 4 times in same st, yrh, pull through all 9 loops on hook.

2trCL (2 treble cluster) – [yrh, insert hook in st, yrh, pull yarn through, yrh, pull through first 2 loops on hook] twice in same st, yrh, pull through all 3 loops on hook.

tr2tog (treble 2 stitches together) – [yrh, insert hook in next sp, yrh, pull yarn through, yrh, pull through first 2 loops on hook] twice, yrh, pull through all 3 loops on hook.

Frdtr (front raised double treble) – st is worked around stem of st in previous round by inserting hook from front around back of st and back through to front as follows: yrh twice, insert hook from front around stem of next st, yrh, pull yarn through, [yrh, pull through first 2 loops on hook] twice, yrh, pull through all 3 loops on hook.

MEASUREMENTS

26cm (10¼in) diameter

TENSION

Centre of Petal-edged Circle (Rounds 1–4) measures 12.5cm (5in) in diameter using 3.5mm (US size E/4) hook and A.

Petal-edged Circle Cloth

Using A, make 6ch, join with a ss in first ch to form a ring.

ROUND 1 (RS): 4ch (counts as 1tr and 1ch), [1tr in ring, 1ch] 15 times, join with a ss in 3rd of first 4ch. (16 stems)
Cont in rounds with RS always facing.

ROUND 2: 5ch (counts as 1tr and first 2ch sp), [1Frdtr around next tr, 2ch, 1tr in next tr, 2ch] 7 times, 1Frdtr around last tr, 2ch, join with a ss in 3rd of first 5ch. (16 stems)

ROUND 3: 3ch (counts as 1tr), *2trCL in top of next Frdtr, 2ch, 1Frdtr around stem of same Frdtr, 2ch, 2trCL in top of same Frdtr as last 2trCL (working behind the Frdtr just made)**, 1tr in next tr; rep from * 6 times more, then once again from * to **, join with a ss in top of first 3ch. (8 Ftrdr groups, 8tr)

ROUND 4: 1ss in sp before next 2trCL, 7ch (counts as 1tr and first 4ch sp), *PS in top of next Frdtr, 5ch**, tr2tog over 2 sps (sp between next 2trCL and next tr and sp between same tr and next tr2tog), 4ch; rep from * 6 times more, then once again from * to **, 1tr in sp between next 2trCL and 3ch, join with a ss in 3rd of 7ch. (8 tr groups, 3 puffs)
Fasten off A.

ROUND 5: Join B with a ss in last ss of last round, 1ch, 1dc in same place as ss, *1ch, 7dtr in next PS, 1ch**, 1dc in next tr2tog; rep from * 6 times more, then once again from * to **, join with a ss in first dc. (8 shells)
Fasten off B.

ROUND 6: Join C with a ss in any 1ch sp to right of any dc, 3ch, miss 1 dc, 1tr in next 1ch sp, *5ch, 1dc in centre dtr of 7dtr shell, 5ch**, tr2tog over next 1ch sp and foll 1ch sp; rep from * 6 times more, then once again from * to **, join with a ss in first tr. (16 ch sps)

ROUND 7: 1ch, 1dc in same place as last ss, *5dc in next 5ch sp, 1dc in next dc, 5dc in 5ch sp, 1dc in next tr2tog; rep from * 6 times more, 5dc in next 5ch sp, 1dc in next dc, 5dc in next 5ch sp, join with a ss in first dc.

ROUND 8: 3ch (counts as 1tr), 2tr in same place, *miss 2 sts, 3tr in next st; rep from * to end, ss in top of first 3ch. (32 tr groups)

ROUND 9: 1ss in each of next 2 tr, 1ss in sp before next 3tr group, 3ch, 2tr in same sp, *3tr in next sp between tr groups; rep from * to end, join with a ss in top of first 3ch. (32 tr groups)

ROUND 10: 1ch, 1dc in same place as last ss, *miss 1 st, 5tr in next st, miss 1 st, 1dc in next st; rep from * to last 3 sts, miss 1 st, 5tr in next st, 1dc in next st, join with a ss in first 1ch. (24 shells)
Fasten off.

Finishing

Sew in ends.
Pin and block cloth to shape.

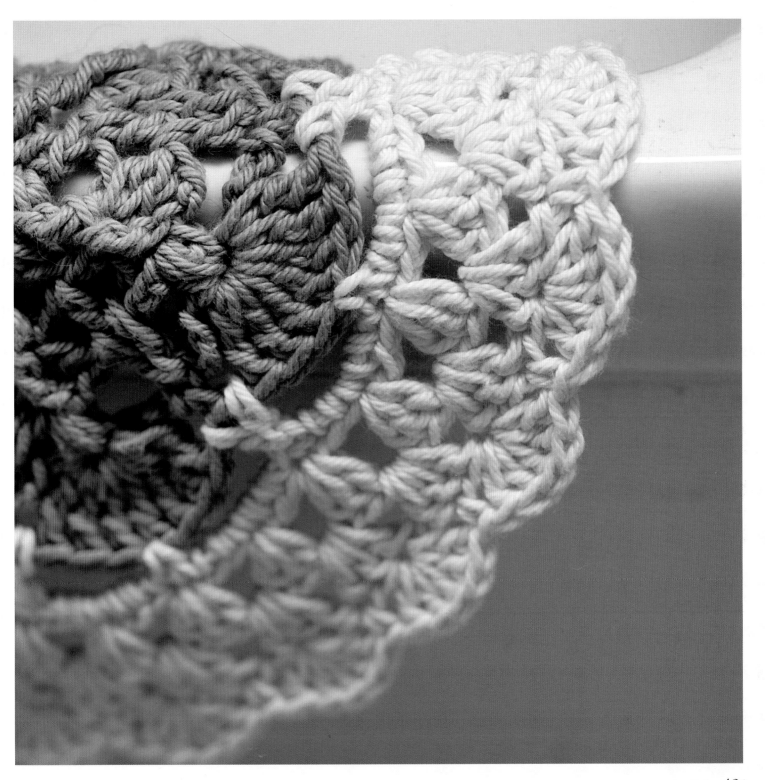

Suppliers

UK Stockists

Laughing Hens
(wool, hooks, accessories)
The Croft Stables
Station Lane
Great Barrow
Cheshire CH3 7JN
01829 740903
www.laughinghens.com

YARN COMPANIES
Rooster Yarns
The Croft Stables
Station Lane
Great Barrow
Cheshire CH3 7JN
01829 740903
www.laughinghens.com

Designer Yarns
(Debbie Bliss yarns)
Units 8-10 Newbridge Industrial Estate
Pitt Street
Keighley
West Yorkshire BD21 4PQ
01535 664222
www.designeryarns.uk.com

Rowan Yarns
Green Lane Mill
Holmfirth
West Yorkshire HD9 2DX
01484 681881
www.knitrowan.com

ACCESSORIES
Debbie Abrahams Beads
26 Church Drive
Nottingham NG5 2BA
0115 855 1799
www.debbieabrahamsbeads.co.uk

Beads Unlimited
PO Box 1
Hove
East Sussex BN3 3SG
mailbox@beadsunlimited.co.uk
01273 740777
www.beadsunlimited.co.uk

TUITION
Nicki Trench Workshops
Crochet, knitting, and craft workshops for all levels.
Email: nicki@nickitrench.com
Blog: nickitrench.blogspot.co.uk

US Stockists

Wool2Dye4
(range of British yarns)
www.wool2dye4.com

Knitting Fever
(Debbie Bliss, Noro and Sirdar yarns)
www.knittingfever.com

The Knitting Garden
(Debbie Bliss, Noro and Sirdar yarns)
www.theknittinggarden.com

Webs
(yarn, hooks, accessories)
www.yarn.com

Yarn Market
(yarn, hooks, accessories)
www.yarnmarket.com

Jo-Ann Fabric and Craft Store
(yarn, hooks, accessories)
1-888-739-4120
www.joann.com

Unicorn Books and Crafts
(hooks, accessories)
www.unicornbooks.com

ACCESSORIES
A.C. Moore
Stores nationwide
1-888-226-6673
www.acmoore.com

Hobby Lobby
Online store and stores nationwide
www.shop.hobbylobby.com
www.hobbylobby.com

Michaels
Stores nationwide
1-800-642-4235
www.michaels.com

Index

Acknowledgements

This book is very much a team effort and I couldn't do without the good-natured commitment and skills of my fantastic group of helpers.

I would particularly like to dedicate this book to my sister-in-law, Mandy Hawes, who is new to my team and whose enthusiasm for crochet has been rekindled recently. Her unending hard work and support led her to making many projects in this book with the kind of commitment that had her crocheting the 100th flower deep into the small hours of the night! Mandy, thanks, I couldn't have done this without you!

My eternal thanks also go to my expert regular team who are reliable, patient and always understand exactly what I want. They are: Carolyn Meggison, Duriye Foley, Sue Lumsden, Pat Cooper and last, but certainly not least, my mum.

Big thanks also to Johnny Okell and Andy Robinson from Rooster Yarns, who are always so generous and quick with their deliveries of wool for the projects; to Rhiannon and Ian from Designer Yarns who kindly supplied Debbie Bliss yarns, to Cara Ackerman from DMC Yarns and also to Rowan Yarns.

Thanks also to Marie Clayton for her reliability and fantastic attention to detail when editing the patterns; to Pete Jorgensen, Carmel Edmonds and Sally Powell at CICO, to Sally Harding for the pattern checking, photographer Caroline Arber and stylist Sophie Martell, and to Louise Turpin for the book design.

Lastly big thanks to Cindy Richards at CICO for commissioning me to write another crochet book and giving me the opportunity to have a great few months producing such lovely crochet projects.